25 AWESOME CARD TRICKS

John Railing

Illustrations by Tony Dunn

THUNDER BAY
P·R·E·S·S

San Diego, California

Thunder Bay Press
An imprint of Printers Row Publishing Group
10350 Barnes Canyon Road, Suite 100, San Diego, CA 92121
www.thunderbaybooks.com

Printers Row Publishing Group is a division of Readerlink Distribution Services, LLC.
Thunder Bay Press is a registered trademark of Readerlink Distribution Services, LLC.

All notations of errors or omissions should be addressed to Thunder Bay Press, Editorial Department, at the above address. All other correspondence (author inquiries, permissions) concerning the content of this book should be addressed to The Book Shop, 7 Peter Cooper Road, #7G, New York, NY 10010, thebookshopltd.com

Thunder Bay Press
Publisher: Peter Norton
Associate Publisher: Ana Parker
Publishing/Editorial Team: April Farr, Kelly Larsen, Kathryn C. Dalby, Carrie Davis
Editorial Team: JoAnn Padgett, Melinda Allman
Production Team: Jonathan Lopes, Rusty von Dyl

Developed by The Book Shop, Ltd.
Designed by Tim Palin Creative
Edited by Susan Lauzau

ISBN: 978-1-68412-424-4

Printed in China

22 21 20 19 18 1 2 3 4 5

DEDICATION

I dedicate this book to the memory of my magic mentors:
Paul Swinford, Harry Riser, Dai Vernon, and Jay Marshall.

CONTENTS

INTRODUCTION

Welcome to *25 Awesome Card Tricks*. Card tricks are the most popular tricks in magic. They are easily performed anywhere you go—for the most part, you only need a deck of cards, though a few tricks in the book use the special "gimmicked" cards included in this kit or simple items like an envelope, pen, and paper. The twenty-five tricks presented here, besides being truly awesome, require no special "moves" or difficult sleight of hand. Instead, they involve subtle techniques and mathematical principles that make the tricks virtually self-working.

Many of the tricks in this book are classics in card magic, while others are novel presentations that will fool even professional magicians. You'll find wonderfully creative approaches to performing magic with cards, along with tips that help you perfect your craft.

Even though the card tricks are relatively easy to perform, you still must practice diligently before presenting them. With the cards in hand, practice until you don't have to think about the sequence of steps. Imagine how you will present the trick; develop your own patter (the talk you use as you perform). Be natural. Do the trick over and over, a hundred times if that's what it takes to feel natural.

If you are unprepared, you likely will expose the trick. If you give away the secret then magic will lose its mystery. You might be tempted to show others how clever you are and tell them how the trick was done, but don't succumb to that temptation. Keep the methods secret. When you are asked, "How'd you do that?" just smile charmingly and say, "I hope you enjoyed it."

In keeping with the secrecy of magic, you should never repeat a trick for the same audience. The first time the spectator sees a trick, there's an element of surprise. When you repeat the trick, the spectator knows what to expect and will look for the secret. It's no longer a trick . . . it's a puzzle to figure out.

CARD AND DECK HANDLING

You should appear at ease when you handle the cards. If you are awkward with a deck or the cards, you will distract your spectators and you will not have the full respect of your audience. When you pick up a deck of cards, you should look as if you know what you're doing.

Hold the deck facedown, in the palm of your left hand, ready for dealing. This is called the *dealer's position* or *mechanic's grip*.

Practice spreading the cards from hand to hand so that your spectator can select a card. From the dealer's position, start pushing the cards to the right with your left thumb. Your right hand comes under the deck palm up, like a tray, ready to receive the cards you just pushed away. Your right thumb holds the top card while your right fingers, under the pack, pull the cards into your palm. This moves the cards from left to right in an orderly, even fashion.

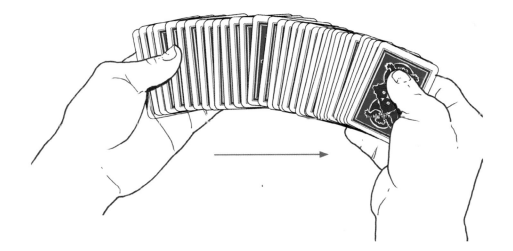

Learn to do a *ribbon spread* to display the cards. This is also called a *table spread* because you are spreading the cards evenly across the table. This move will come in handy for endings for some tricks. First, you need the proper surface on the table to do this well—the surface can't be too slippery. You'll soon learn which surfaces work well. The ribbon spread is easier to do when the cards are in fairly new condition.

With the deck on the table, position your right hand so that your index finger is on the left side of the deck, your thumb is on the inner end, and your fingers are on the outer end. This is where the feel or knack of card handling comes in. Slide the entire pack to your right, gently lifting your index finger. The result is an even spread of cards across the table. Your forefinger does the work.

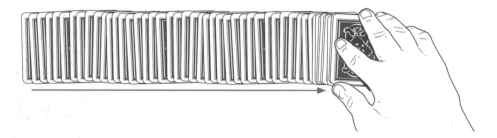

Finally, practice doing a *riffle-shuffle*. Place the cards horizontally on the table in front of you. Your right hand cuts the top section in half, placing the cards immediately to the right of the original deck. Your thumbs are behind the *packets* (a packet refers to any group of cards less than the full deck) and your middle fingers are in front (a). Turn both packets so that they form a small "V" shape on the table (b). Your two thumbs lift the corners of the cards off the table along the inner edges. Allow the cards to interlace as you relax pressure on your thumbs (c). Then move both hands away from the center, toward the outer edge, and push the two halves together, squaring the cards with your fingers (d).

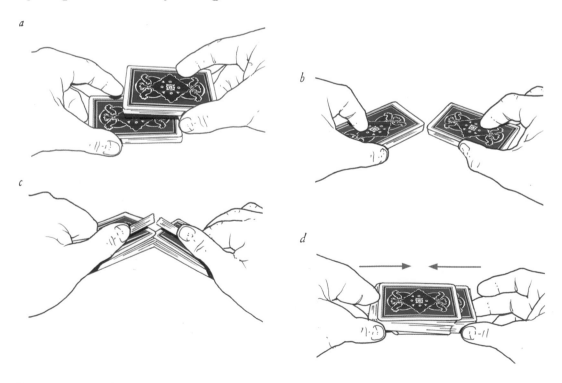

FAKE OR FALSE SHUFFLING

There are several tricks in the book that require a *setup*, a stack of cards placed on the top or bottom of the deck in advance of the trick. You need to be able to shuffle the deck without disturbing the setup. The riffle-shuffle is ideal for doing this. Assume that you have a setup on top of the deck. All you need to do is control the shuffle so that the top cards, when you come to them, are held back as the left-hand cards interlace beneath them. In other words, you let all the left-hand cards fall before the last group in your right hand.

Similarly, if the setup is on the bottom of the deck, at the start of your shuffle allow the left-hand cards to fall first—before you start to interlace them. See illustration c of the riffle-shuffle to get a sense of how you can let cards fall before interlacing them.

When performing tricks that require a stack on top, it's very important to shuffle the deck first, keeping the cards on top with the riffle. This eliminates, in the spectator's mind, the possibility that the cards are arranged. For tricks that involve a setup of cards, handle the deck normally and don't worry that someone will notice. People will assume the deck is well mixed—one false riffle-shuffle is all you need to do. You can turn the deck faceup to show that the cards are mixed. Most of the time, the setup will be on the top or on the bottom of the deck. It's easy to spread the cards so as not to show the setup.

TRICK TYPES

I've included a variety of card tricks in this book, and most of them fall into four main categories of effects:

- **PICK-A-CARD TRICKS.** These are the card tricks familiar to most people, and I've featured ten of them in the book. In seven of these, the spectator freely selects a card, and then you control the card or otherwise determine where it is before revealing it. In three of the tricks, the spectator does not have a free choice (you will "force him" to pick a certain card).

- **FOUR-ACE TRICKS.** This is a big category in magic. In these tricks, the magician finds the four Aces, or Aces are the featured cards. There are four tricks of this type in the book. You don't have to use the four Aces, though; you could substitute the four Kings, for example.

- **POKER-THEMED TRICKS.** In this category of tricks, the presentation usually involves dealing hands of cards, with the magician getting the winning hand or ending up with a royal flush. There are six poker-themed tricks in the book.

- **PREDICTION TRICKS.** In several of the five prediction-related tricks included in the book, the prediction is written in advance and sealed in an envelope. You should be creative when writing the prediction. For example, if you know the spectator will be your friend Bob, instead of simply writing the name of the card, write "Bob will select the Four of Hearts" (or whatever card you select). You could also give the prediction to the spectator in advance, with instructions not to open the envelope until instructed to do so when you perform the effect.

The *effect* is what the audience perceives or experiences; the technique used to create that effect is called the *method*. This is the secret. Rather than relying on difficult sleight of hand, these tricks use other methods (such as forcing, using key cards, or utilizing prearranged setups). In several tricks, the method involves a subtle use of mathematics.

CARD CONTROL AND REVELATION

Many card tricks involve "controlling" a selected card. You might not know what this card is but you know where it is (the location of the card in the deck). Selections are generally controlled to the top or bottom of the deck, in readiness for the *revelation*.

I refer to the revelation many times in this book. The techniques you employ in the trick (forcing a card or using math) are part of the hidden method. The spectator should not be aware of them. However, the revelation is paramount. Great card revelations can be reputation makers. Depending on the trick, the revelation might involve the spectator opening up an envelope with a prediction inside, the name of the selected card magically appearing on the magician's forearm, or the spectator finding the chosen card himself. Don't simply turn over the card at the end and ask, "Is that your card?" In almost every trick you perform, you should have the spectator announce his card just before you turn it over to show it.

TERMINOLOGY

Playing cards have *backs* and *faces*. These terms should be obvious. The back, or *top*, is the ornate back design of the card. The face, or *bottom*, is where you'd look to see what the card is—the Queen of Hearts or Two of Spades, for example. The deck also has a top and bottom. If the deck is facedown in your hand, the top card is the first one on the top of the deck, as you might expect. And the bottom card is the last one, next to your palm. If you turn the deck over so that it is faceup in your hand, the top card and bottom card didn't change: the top card is now underneath the deck, and you are looking at the face of the bottom card.

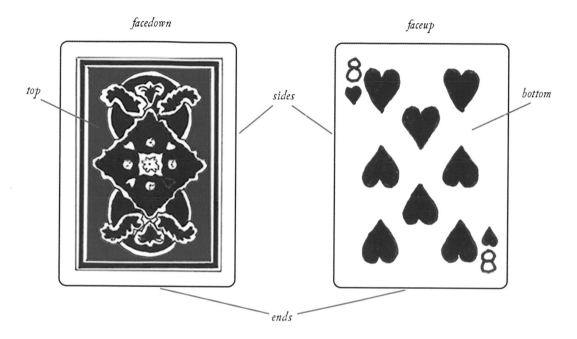

facedown

faceup

top

sides

bottom

ends

COURT CARD: a playing card that is a Jack, Queen, or King of any suit

EFFECT: what the trick looks like to the spectator; what the audience sees

INDIFFERENT CARD: any card used in a trick with an identity that is unimportant to the trick; a card that is not the focus of a trick

FORCE OR CARD FORCE ("FORCING A CARD"): controlling the spectator's selection without him or her knowing it; the opposite of a "freely selected card"

GIMMICKED CARD OR GIMMICK CARD: a special, nonstandard card that is used in tricks without the audience's knowledge; also called *gaffed* cards or simply *gaffs*. (Two gimmicked cards are supplied with this kit: the double-faced card, which has faces on both sides, and the double-backed card, which has a back design on both sides.)

GLIMPSE: a secret or non-obvious glance at a card. (If I ask you to glimpse the bottom card, for example, you might tilt the deck a little and take a quick look. This could then become a key card.)

KEY CARD: a card whose identity you know that will indicate the spectator's selection; typically, the key card ends up next to the spectator's card, and thus, when you spot the key, then you know the card the spectator selected

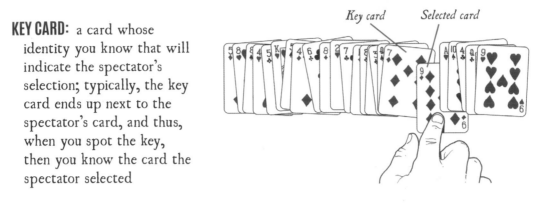

Key card   Selected card

MISDIRECTION: the art of having spectators look at something other than the thing you don't want them to see, such as secretly turning over a deck. (A ploy all magicians use is to simply ask the spectator a question, such as: "Do you remember your card?" Spectators will invariably look at the questioner and away from the cards for a brief moment as they answer.)

MOVE: a secret manipulation, often referred to as a *sleight* (as in "sleight of hand")

PATTER: the talk used during the performance of the trick; it's what you say as you're performing. (I've suggested patter in some places, to get you started, but you should change the patter to fit your style. There are some tricks where the patter is crucial for the presentation, for example, Lie Detector and Further Than That.)

SETUP: a secret prearrangement of a group of cards in the deck, also referred to as a *stack* (as in "stacking the deck"); the stack could involve only a few cards or the entire deck

SPOT CARD: a playing card with its rank indicated by symbols, or "spots," on its face; these are the Ace through Ten

GETTING STARTED

Each trick begins with a description of the effect. Then I tell you what you need (usually just a deck of cards), along with the secret and any setup that is required. Step-by-step instructions follow, together with illustrations that highlight critical moments or techniques in the trick.

Tricks are arranged so that the easiest ones are toward the beginning, and the more difficult or sophisticated tricks are in the second half. Start with the simpler ones and move through the book at your own pace. After perfecting several of the tricks, consider how you might combine multiple effects into a routine. By the time you reach the end of the book, you will have gained the skill and confidence to wow any audience!

THE
TRICKS

KINGS AND ACES

This is a simple—but awesome—card trick with a double ending. You really don't have to do anything except set up a few cards ahead of time—just give the instructions to the spectator, and he or she does all the work.

EFFECT: The spectator is instructed to deal some cards into two piles and then deal those into four piles. You show that there's a King on top of each of the four piles. Just when he thought the trick was over, you have the spectator turn over the four Aces!

NEEDED: A deck of cards.

SECRET AND SETUP: The secret is in the setup. Before the beginning of the trick, you secretly stack the deck (you are going to arrange twelve cards on top). From the top of the deck down, place four indifferent cards (it doesn't matter what they are), then the four Kings, then the four Aces, then the rest of the deck.

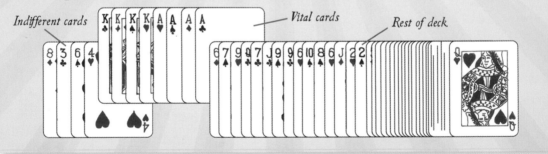

STEP 1. Tell the spectator that you are going to demonstrate what you would like him to do. The deck of cards with the twelve-card setup on top is facedown in your hand (dealer's position). Start dealing the top cards, one at a time, alternately into two piles side by side on the table. You can start on the left or right; it doesn't matter. Deal two cards onto each pile (a total of four cards). Then stop.

STEP 2. Gather or scoop up the four cards you just dealt and put them on the *bottom* of the deck. You've now shown what you want the spectator to do and, at the same time, eliminated the four indifferent cards. Now the Kings are on top of the deck. You could do this trick without using the four indifferent cards and simply start with the next step. But this way is much better.

STEP 3. Hand the deck to the spectator. Say, "Take the pack and deal down two piles, as I just did." Allow the spectator to deal about a dozen cards or so (at least eight), then tell him, "You may stop at any time you wish." When the spectator stops dealing, say, "Are you satisfied? You can keep dealing, if you'd like, or remove a few cards." Take back the rest of the deck and put it aside; you won't need it.

STEP 4. The Kings and Aces are on the bottom of these two piles. You need the spectator to deal these two piles again to get these cards to the top. Ask the spectator to pick either pile and deal that out into two piles, just as he did before.

STEP 5. After the spectator is finished separating the first pile, have him divide the other pile into two smaller piles in the same way, by dealing alternately. Now you will have four piles of about equal number, side by side. There's a King on top of each pile, with an Ace directly under each one.

STEP 6. It's now time for the revelation, the awesome double ending. Remind the spectator that he dealt as many cards as he desired, and then divided those cards into four piles. Slowly reveal the top card of each pile to show the Kings, flipping each backward and placing it behind its pile. After the second King is revealed, say, "Isn't that a coincidence—two Kings!" Act surprised at each King.

STEP 7. Don't rush into the revelation of the Aces. Give the spectator a few seconds to appreciate finding the four Kings. He probably thinks this is it. Say, "Are you a poker player? What beats four Kings? Four Aces? Right!" Make a magical wave over the cards and ask the spectator to turn over the top card of each pile. Awesome!

LIE DETECTOR

This awesome card trick involves only seven cards.
It is self-working (it requires no special magical skills).

EFFECT: The spectator picks a card from among seven cards, remembers it, and returns it to the group. You tell the spectator that you will determine what the card is by asking four questions about the card, for example, its color and its value. At first, the spectator wonders what the trick is if she tells you. But . . . you tell her that she can lie or tell the truth. You spell out her answers while dealing a card for each letter. Even though the spectator may have lied about her answers, you find the card.

NEEDED: Any seven cards from the deck.

SECRET: The secret to this trick is a very subtle use of mathematics—but no calculation is required.

STEP 1. Remove any seven cards from the deck. I like to include a mix of red and black cards, but the particular selection really doesn't matter. Put the deck aside; you won't need it.

STEP 2. Fan the seven cards facedown and ask the spectator to choose a card, look at it, and remember it. Keep the cards fanned.

STEP 3. You want the card returned so that it will be positioned third from the top. Don't try to hide this, just perform the action as if it doesn't matter. After the spectator looks at her card, separate the top two cards from the fanned cards with your right hand. Extend your left hand with its four cards and have the spectator replace her card on top (a). Drop or add back on top the two cards from the right hand (b). Again, this is done very casually, as if the cards' placement doesn't matter. The card will now be in the correct position, third from the top.

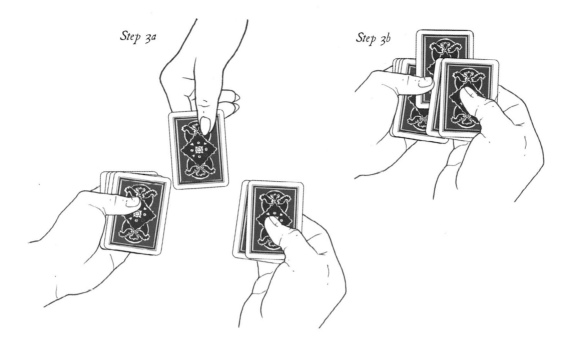

Step 3a

Step 3b

STEP 4: Say, "I am going to try to determine the identity of your card. I have to ask you a few questions about it, such as its color, its suit, and its value." Pause here a second or two for the absurdity to register. "But . . . you can lie or you can tell the truth! After each response, I will spell your answer, further mixing the cards."

STEP 5: Hold the packet of seven cards in your left hand. Ask the first question: "Was your card red or black? You can lie or tell the truth." After the spectator responds, you spell her answer, dealing one card onto the table for each letter. Thus, if the spectator says her card is red, you deal three cards onto the table, spelling, out loud, "R – E – D" as you do. Then drop the balance (in this case, four cards) on top. If the spectator says her card is black, you deal five cards, spelling out loud "B-L-A-C-K" as you do, then drop the balance (in this case, two cards) on top. This method of spelling and dropping the remaining cards on top will be repeated for each answer.

STEP 6: Pick up the packet of seven cards and continue with the second question: "What was the suit of your card? Again, you can lie or tell the truth." As before, no matter what the answer is, you deal one card for each letter, spelling out loud. And, as before, you drop the balance of the cards on top of the dealt cards. One caveat here: it is important that if the spectator says, "Clubs," that you include the "s" in the spelling. Incidentally, there aren't enough cards to spell out Diamonds with the final "s." So, if the spectator says Diamonds, you only spell "D-I-A-M-O-N-D," and there won't be any cards left to drop on top. This is okay. (It doesn't matter whether you include the "s" if you spell Hearts or Spades. I usually don't include the "s" so that I can drop at least two cards on top after spelling.)

STEP 7: Pick up the packet of seven cards and continue with the third question: "Now for the value of your card. What was the value or rank? Remember, you can lie or tell the truth." It doesn't matter what the spectator says (she could even say "deuce" instead of "two"), you spell the answer, calling out each letter as you deal the cards onto the table. Then drop the balance on top.

STEP 8: Pick up the packet of seven cards and continue with the fourth question: "Just one more question. Were your answers lies, true, or both?" Pause here for a second, then say, "And you can lie about this, too!" In other words, the spectator can lie about whether she lied. And, as before, you will deal and spell, and drop the balance on top. If the spectator says her answers were true, for example, you would spell "T-R-U-E" and then drop the remaining cards on top. Note that each of these possible answers contains four letters, so you will end up in the same position with whatever answer the spectator gives you ("lies" or "true" or "both").

STEP 9: After all of this dealing and spelling, the selected card is now on top of the packet of seven cards on the table. Pick up the top card (don't turn it over yet). Say, "Now, honestly this time, what was the name of your card?" After the spectator answers, turn the card over.

 How does this trick work? Try practicing it with the selected card faceup. You will see that the selected card starts third from the top, then moves to third from the bottom, then back to third from the top. The card simply shuttles back and forth throughout the trick to one of two locations. For the last question, because the three possible answers have the same number of letters (four), you will end up with the selection on top, ready for the revelation.

COUNT DOWN FIVE

In this awesome trick, you seem to make a mistake when finding a selected card. Of course, you *will* find the right card, along with a surprising ending.

EFFECT: A card is selected and replaced in the deck. You state that you will cause the selected card to magically turn over, so that it is faceup. However, it appears that you make a mistake, because the wrong card is faceup (a five-spot). You use the five-spot to count down five cards and find the selected card. The trick seems to be over, but then you reveal the four Aces!

NEEDED: A deck of cards.

SECRET AND SETUP: This is a trick that requires a setup—a group of five cards: a reversed five-spot and the four Aces. This group of five cards is on the bottom of the deck. Remove any five-spot and the four Aces from the deck. Reverse the five-spot and put it faceup on the bottom of the deck. Then put the four Aces facedown below this. The situation is that the deck is facedown except for one card (the five-spot), which is near the bottom, with only the four Aces beneath it.

Four Aces

STEP 1. Bring out the deck and have the spectator select a card. In doing so, be sure that you don't spread the cards all the way and reveal the faceup five-spot near the bottom.

STEP 2. After the spectator has selected and memorized a card, it will be replaced so that it ends up directly below this group of five cards. You will do this with a series of small cuts as follows:

a. With the deck in your left hand, cut small packets of cards from the top and place them on the table in one pile. As you are doing this, ask the spectator to replace her card anytime on the pile as you are removing small packets and placing them on the table.

b. When the spectator places her card on the pile, simply drop the balance of the deck on top of this card.

c. The situation now is that the selected card is just below the five-card setup.

STEP 3. The rest of the trick is basically all acting (and counting of cards). Tell the spectator that you will magically cause her card to turn over. Make a magic gesture with the deck: either shake the deck or riffle the corners.

STEP 4. Spread the deck facedown on the table (ribbon spread), showing the five-spot faceup. Pretend to be very satisfied because you caused the supposed selected card to turn over. The spectator will state that this is not her card. Act bewildered: "I wonder why it's faceup, then." Continue: "It must have turned over for a reason." Pause. "It must mean that we should count down five cards."

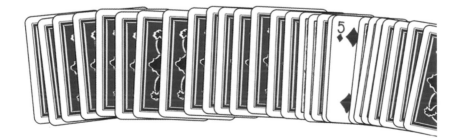

STEP 5. Now separate the cards at the five-spot (better for the upcoming revelation). Move the five-spot aside and count very deliberately and carefully, sliding each of the four cards into its own group, then stop while holding the fifth card facedown. This will be the selected card, but don't reveal it yet.

STEP 6. Ask for the name of the selected card before turning it over (always a good idea—it makes for a better revelation). Then turn over the fifth card to show this is the one selected (the Eight of Spades, in this example).

STEP 7. Now for the surprise ending. Act as if the trick is finished. After a brief pause, continue: "But if you were playing poker, you'd need a hand of five cards." Pick up the four facedown Aces (which had been counted) and turn them over, adding them to the selected card. "And this would be a winning hand."

INFLUENTIAL CARDS

This is a bold, perplexing "quickie" that is easy to
do when you are asked to perform a card trick.

EFFECT: The spectator cuts the deck into two halves. You look at the top card of the
bottom half; it tells you the identity of the top card of the other half. You repeat this
quick trick a few times. For the finale, you call out the names of the top cards on both
halves!

NEEDED: A deck of cards.

SECRET: You have glimpsed the top card of the deck beforehand.

STEP 1. Have the spectator shuffle the deck and hand it to you. Secretly look at and
remember the top card. You can also do this boldly: spread the cards faceup to show
that the cards are truly mixed, and glance at the top card. Then close up the spread
and turn the deck facedown.

STEP 2. Hold your left hand
with your palm up, parallel
to the floor. Place the deck
facedown squarely on the
palm of your outstretched left
hand, close to your thumb.
Ask the spectator to cut the
deck in half, placing the
top half next to the bottom
half. The spectator places
the cut-off top half on your
fingers. If you find it difficult
to balance both halves on your
outstretched hand, use the
table instead.

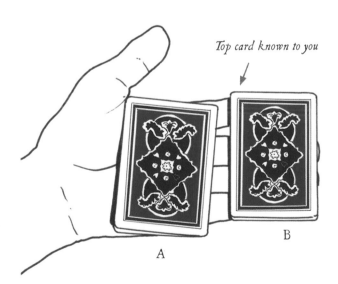

Top card known to you

A

B

STEP 3. The half on your fingers, closest to the spectator (B), has the "known" card on top. Look at the card on the top half nearest you (A). Say, "By looking at this card, I can tell you the name of the card on top of the other pile." Remember the card you just picked up, and call out the name of the first "glimpsed" card. (You have to do two things at once here. You are calling out the name of the first card while remembering the name of a new card.) Replace the card you just looked at. The spectator turns over the card on top of pile B and sees that you are correct.

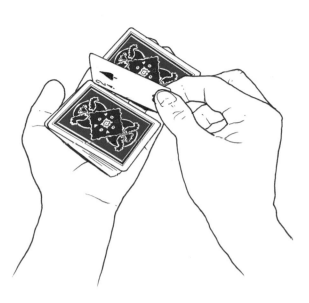

STEP 4. After the spectator replaces her card, complete the cut by taking the half nearest you and placing it on top of the other one. You now know the name of the top card and can repeat the trick. Do this a few more times (not too many, though). Each time, you look at (and remember) the card on the pile nearest you (A) and name the top card of the other pile (B). This is a concept in magic called the "one-ahead principle." You can see why. Using the one-ahead principle, a basic technique in mentalism, you can make seemingly impossible predictions and perform some very convincing mind reading. This principle is a very old one, first appearing in a written description in 1723.

STEP 5. The last time you do the trick, announce, "I will now name the top cards of both piles!" You are going to do something quite audacious. Point to the top card of packet A and call out the glimpsed-at card from just before. Now take the top card from packet A with your right hand; lift it off the deck so only you can see it. Get a quick peek at this card, but do not show it. Without pausing, point to the top of B and say, "And that card is the (name of the card you just lifted off packet A that you have in your hand)." Lift the card off the top of B with your right hand, which is holding the other card, add it to the first card, and drop them both faceup on the table. All this happens quickly and smoothly. You actually miscall the cards. The spectator will have no idea that these were miscalled.

TURN ABOUT

This is a baffling effect that is both startling and mind-boggling. You will be credited with great skill.

EFFECT: The spectator cuts off half the deck and selects any card from his half. You select a card from your half. You each replace your cards in the other person's packet. The two halves are combined in a faceup and facedown manner. Instantly, you cause the cards to turn the same direction, except for the two selected cards.

NEEDED: A deck of cards.

SECRET AND SETUP: You know the bottom card. To prepare, you reverse the deck and then secretly turn over the bottom card so that it is faceup in the facedown deck. You will also do a sneaky turnover of the deck while the spectator is not looking (misdirection).

STEP 1. If you haven't done this beforehand, secretly look at the bottom card, remember it, and reverse it so that it is faceup under the facedown deck. Let's assume that this card is the Five of Hearts. With the deck facedown in your left hand, spread the top cards so that your spectator can see them, then square them up again.

STEP 2. Extend the deck to the spectator and say, "Please cut off about half of the deck. Shuffle your cards. Pull one card out of the center, look at it, and remember it. I'll do the same." Go through the motions of pulling a card from the center of your packet and looking at it, but there's no reason to remember it. Just disregard this card.

STEP 3. Say, "I'll place my card in your half." Push your card into the center of the spectator's packet. At the same time, drop your left hand to your side so that the deck is out of sight for a moment. Turn it over so that the reversed card is on top of the deck when you bring your hand up again. You do this very naturally as you are placing your card into the spectator's half of the deck. This is called misdirection: the spectator will be paying attention to you inserting your card into his packet and not paying attention to your left hand, which has naturally dropped down and is turning the deck over. If you are seated, you can drop your left hand to your lap for a moment and turn the deck over.

STEP 4. Say, "May I have your card, please?" Take the spectator's card and push it facedown into the center of your half of the deck. (The half is really faceup, with the exception of the topmost card.) Say, "Now, please give me about half of your packet of cards. I'll turn it over and place it on top of these cards." Reverse the cards he gives you and place them on your packet so that about one third of your cards are protruding forward. Say, "May I have the rest of your cards?" Turn these upside down and place them behind your stack faceup, so that another third is showing.

STEP 5. Now push all the cards together, squaring up the deck. It appears that some cards are upside down, while others are not. Say, "I shall attempt to turn all the cards over so that they face in one direction—except for our selected cards. My card was the Five of Hearts (name the card that was originally reversed on the bottom of the deck). What was yours?" The spectator names his card.

STEP 6. After the spectator names his card, spread all the cards facedown in a ribbon spread across the table. All cards will be facing the same direction, except for the two cards named, your reversed card and the spectator's chosen card.

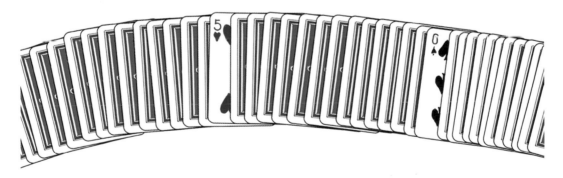

 An alternate revelation is to ribbon spread the deck faceup at the end. All the cards will be faceup except two facedown cards, which are neatly spaced within the spread. Let the spectator remove these and turn them over to show that they are, indeed, the selected cards.

AWESOME PREDICTION

Your prediction of a card is sealed in an envelope. Of course, you will be correct!

EFFECT: You hand the spectator a sealed envelope containing a prediction. The spectator cuts and removes some cards from the deck, and you deal out a row of cards. A card is selected based on the number of cards the spectator removed. Then the envelope is opened and the prediction read: "This evening, the Nine of Hearts will be selected" (or any other card you choose). The card is turned over and matches your prediction.

NEEDED: A deck of cards, an envelope, a piece of paper, and a pen or pencil.

SECRET AND SETUP: The predicted card is in the twenty-first position from the top of the deck. Math does the rest. (The card doesn't have to be the Nine of Hearts—this is just the example.) To set up the card trick, write the name of your chosen card on the piece of paper and seal it in the envelope. When the time comes to do the trick, be sure that the predicted card is twenty-first from the top of the deck.

STEP 1. Bring out the sealed prediction. Hand the envelope to the spectator to keep. (See the tip on page 26 for ideas to make your prediction more sensational.)

STEP 2. Set the deck on the table. Turn to the spectator and say, "I need help for this trick. Please cut off a small group of cards, about a quarter of the pack or so, and hold on to those cards until we need them." (Please note that if the spectator cuts more than twenty cards, the trick will not work. You need to be alert here. Watch carefully as the spectator cuts the cards. If you feel that the spectator may have cut too many cards, stop him and say, "Don't cut so many . . . just a small group of cards off the top of the deck." If the spectator happens to cut half the deck, for example, you might say, "We don't need so many . . . drop about half of those back on top of the deck." This is an example of what is referred to as "spectator management." You emphasize the adjective "small" and monitor the cutting. It's quite all right to stop the spectator and have him cut a smaller group.)

STEP 3. Pick up the remainder of the pack and begin to deal cards onto the table from right to left. Make sure each card overlaps the one before it. Each card should be showing. Deal twenty cards and stop.

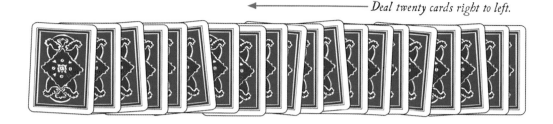

← Deal twenty cards right to left.

STEP 4. Say to the spectator, "You don't know how many cards you have there, do you? Please count your cards." After the spectator counts them, you can have someone else verify the count, if you'd like. This ensures that there are no mistakes in counting.

STEP 5. Assume that the spectator has twelve cards. Say, "Twelve! Okay, let's count twelve cards." Start counting cards from *left to right*, stopping on the twelfth card. Push it out of the spread, keeping it facedown.

Count left to right. ———————————→

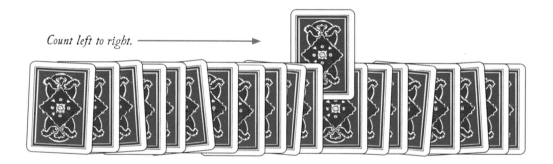

STEP 6. Say, "We came to this card strictly by chance. We had no idea how many cards you were going to cut to. Please bring out the envelope that you have kept all along. I will not touch it. Please open it and read what's inside." The spectator will read the prediction made earlier.

STEP 7. Have the spectator turn over the card that was set aside. Voila!

 There are several effects in the book where you predict a card that will be selected. You could simply write your prediction, fold the slip of paper, and put it aside to be read at the end of the trick. However, you could do much more to create greater impact. Ideally, the prediction should be sealed in an envelope. This adds to the anticipation as the spectator opens the envelope and removes the prediction.

The revelation is even better if you have the prediction already written and sealed in an envelope before the trick begins. On arrival to a friend's house for a party, hand the host the envelope. Ask her to sign her name across the flap and to put the envelope in a prominent place. If you know the name of one of the guests, you might have written "John Smith will select the Nine of Hearts," for example. Just before the revelation of the selected card, point to the envelope and say, "That envelope has been sitting on that mantel the entire evening. I have not touched it since my arrival when I asked our host to sign it. Please verify that it is still sealed and has not been tampered with. Would you please open it and read the contents?" The focus is not on the relatively simple technique of forcing the selected card—the emphasis is on the envelope and the prediction.

SPECTATOR CUTS THE ACES

Four-Ace tricks are very popular with magicians. It's most awesome when the spectator does the work and finds the Aces!

EFFECT: Although the magician never touches the deck, the spectator cuts it into four piles and mixes up the cards—and the top card on each pile is found to be an Ace.

NEEDED: A deck of cards.

SECRET AND SETUP: The secret is the positioning of the Aces in advance of the trick. To set up the trick, find the four Aces and move them to the top of the deck.

STEP 1. After (secretly) getting the four Aces to the top of the deck, place the deck on the table and ask the spectator to cut it into two approximately equal halves. Keep track of the original top of the deck at all times (that is, the packet with the four Aces on top).

STEP 2. Ask the spectator to cut one of the packets in half again, and place them side by side.

STEP 3. Ask for the other half-deck to be cut in half again, in the opposite direction, indicating with your hand where the final packet should go. (Make sure you still know which pile has the four Aces on top.)

STEP 4. You should have four approximately equal packets in front of you. The four Aces should be on the top of one of the end packets, depending on which way the cards were cut. Point out that the spectator has now found four random points in the deck.

STEP 5. Point to the packet at the opposite end to the Aces. Let's assume the Aces are in the pile on the right. Ask the spectator to pick up the packet on the far left and to move three cards from the top to the bottom. The fact that the spectator makes all the moves increases the apparent fairness of the whole procedure.

Spectator moves three cards from top to bottom.

STEP 6. Now tell the spectator to deal one card from the top of the packet in her hand onto each of the piles on the table, in any order she wishes.

Spectator deals a card to the top of each pile.

STEP 7. Have the spectator replace the first packet to the same spot on the table, then pick up the second packet and repeat the same procedure; that is, she takes three cards from the top and places them at the bottom. Then ask her to deal one card to the top of each pile on the table.

STEP 8. This exact sequence should be repeated with the third packet. Each time, explain which moves to make and watch to ensure that the spectator follows your instructions correctly.

STEP 9. The fourth packet is treated in exactly the same way. This will result in four facedown packets, which you have not touched from the very beginning.

STEP 10. Emphasize the randomness of the cuts and that the spectator has mixed the cards further.

STEP 11. For the revelation: turn over one of the cards on the top of one of the packets. It will be an Ace. Pause. Then turn over the top cards of the remaining three packets, revealing an Ace on each.

 Why does this work? During the sequence of movements, what actually happens is that you add three cards on top of the Aces, and then move those three added cards to the bottom and deal one Ace to each of the other three piles. All the other moves are simply a smokescreen to help hide the method!

WANNA BET?

This is simple to do. It's a good one for laughs, but still an amazing discovery of a selected card.

EFFECT: A card is selected and replaced in the deck. You deal through the cards faceup in an attempt to find the card. However, you pass it by and continue dealing, stopping a few cards later. You then make the bold statement that the next card you turn over will be the selection. Of course, the spectator assumes that this will be impossible (as the card has already been passed). She may even want to bet you! However, you win the bet because you actually reach in and turn her card facedown.

NEEDED: A deck of cards.

SECRET: You use a "key card" to know the location of the spectator's card. This key card is on the bottom of the deck at the beginning of the trick. The key card will end up adjacent to the selected card, so you know which one it is.

STEP 1. Glimpse the bottom card of the deck and remember it. Don't be obvious about this glimpse.

Step 1

STEP 2. Hand the deck to the spectator and ask her to cut the deck into three even piles.

STEP 3. Have the spectator take a card from the middle of any pile and look at it. After looking at it, have her replace it on top of any other pile. You now put the piles together, making sure that the key card will go on top of the selected card. (If the spectator puts the card on top of the pile containing the key, ask her to cut the pile and replace the cut. This will do the same thing, putting the key on top of the selected card.)

STEP 4. After the deck is reassembled, you can cut the deck if you choose. You will now deal the cards, one at a time, turning each one faceup as you deal. Say, "I am going to try to find your card . . . don't say anything or give me any indication which one is your card." You want to deal the cards so that they are overlapping, in a row, so the spectator can see the faces.

STEP 5. As you deal the cards faceup, look for the key card (the Seven of Diamonds, in this case). When you see it, you will know that the next card following this will be the selection. After seeing the selected card, forget the key card and memorize the selected card instead. Continue dealing but do not change your pattern of dealing—just keep going. Make sure part of the selected card is visible in the upturned cards. After several cards, slow your dealing as if you sense you are coming to the selection. Then stop, holding a card in your hand as if to turn it over.

STEP 6. Say (with confidence), "I'll make you a bet that the next card I turn over will be your card." The spectator will generally be delighted to make this bet, as she knows you have passed her card already. And, she believes you are going to turn over the card in your hand.

STEP 7. Once the bet is made, you proceed to reach down and remove the selection (a) and turn it facedown (b).

Step 7a

Step 7b

To avoid arguments, don't make this a real money bet. The trick is just for fun.

CHEATING AT CARDS

You will probably be asked if you can cheat at cards. Here is a perfect trick that makes it appear as if you have great skill at card cheating. This is simple to do because it's automatic.

EFFECT: You give a demonstration of cheating at cards, dealing out five poker hands of five cards each. You show how you can deal yourself the four Aces from the bottom of the deck. You repeat this, and end up with a royal flush!

NEEDED: A deck of cards.

SECRET AND SETUP: The secret is a little setup at the beginning, in which you place the Ten, Jack, Queen, and King of Spades on top of the deck. When you deal the cards for the first part of the demonstration, you are setting up for the second part, with the royal flush cards in the required positions, every fifth card. It's mathematical but so subtle that even magicians don't realize the method.

STEP 1. Take the deck with the secret setup on top and spread the cards with the faces toward you. Say, "Let me show you how a card shark can cheat at cards. First, you need to find the four Aces." Spread the deck faceup in your hands and look for the four

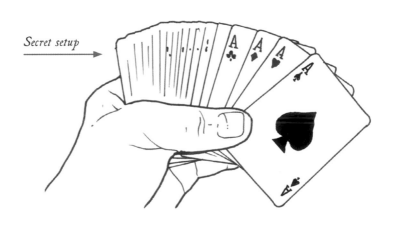

Secret setup

Aces. When you come to the Aces, slip them to the face, or bottom, of the deck, with the Ace of Spades on the very bottom. You do this openly, but don't spread the cards at the very top of the deck and reveal the setup.

STEP 2. Holding the deck faceup, spread the bottom four cards to display the four Aces, as shown in the Step 1 illustration. Remember that the Ace of Spades must be at the face.

STEP 3. Say, "The card shark can cheat using a technique called 'bottom dealing.' The cards he desires are on the bottom of the deck, and he has the skill to deal those cards to himself without the other players noticing. This takes a lot of practice." Square up the deck and turn it facedown, holding it in the dealing position in

your left hand. You are going to demonstrate "bottom dealing." Continue, "Let's say there are five poker players, and the card shark is dealing." Deal a five-handed round of poker, dealing the last card to yourself. You deal regularly to the other four hands. But, when you deal to yourself, you openly take the card for your hand from the bottom of the deck as you say, "Here is where the card shark does the bottom deal. I'm not good at it, but you can see how the card shark can deal himself the Aces." Remember, you're giving a demonstration, so it doesn't have to be deceptive.

STEP 4. Repeat the deal four more times, so each poker hand ends up with five cards in it. Deal the first four hands normally, then deal your card from the bottom very deliberately each time.

STEP 5. Turn over your poker hand to display the four Aces, along with one other card behind them. The other hands remain facedown. Say, "And the card shark ends up with the four Aces, beating the other players."

STEP 6. Pick up your poker hand, turn it facedown, and drop it on top of the balance of the deck in your left hand. With your right hand, gather the remaining four hands. Just drop each hand one on top of the other in any order and then drop the gathered hands on top of the deck.

STEP 7. Say, "Now I'll deal the cards again. See if you can spot my bottom dealing." As before, deal the five-handed round of poker, dealing five cards to each hand; you get the last card of each round. But this time, you don't have to demonstrate the obvious bottom deal. Just deal normally off the top of the deck.

STEP 8. After you have dealt the hands, say, "Let's take a look at the hands." Turn the other four poker hands faceup and spread them. You might comment about what's in the hands—a pair or two pairs or whatever. Three of the hands will have an Ace in them. Observant spectators may believe that this demonstration is not going to work because those Aces should be in your hand.

STEP 9. Say, "To guarantee you will win, you need the best hand." Turn over your hand and spread the cards. "A royal flush!"

FOLLOW THE LEADER

This is not a "pick-a-card" trick, and you don't need
the entire deck for this trick—only twelve cards. But it's awesome!

EFFECT: Five red-suited cards and five black-suited cards are placed on the table in two separate packets. Then so-called leader cards are placed in front of the packets, with the proper color aligned. However, when the leader cards are switched, the cards in the packets appear to follow the leaders according to color.

NEEDED: Twelve cards: six red-suited cards and six black-suited cards.

SECRET: A special cut and a little psychology combine to fool the spectator.

STEP 1. Remove twelve cards from the deck: six red cards and six black cards. Place the deck aside. The twelve cards are faceup in your left hand.

STEP 2. Say, "You know the saying that 'birds of a feather flock together'? Well, likewise, cards of a color like to associate with cards of the same color." Place a black card faceup on the table. Then place a red card faceup to the right of the black card. Explain that these will be the leader cards.

STEP 3. Sort the other ten faceup cards so that the five black cards are behind the five red cards. In other words, you have a packet of ten cards, faceup, with the red cards showing on the face.

This trick uses a sleight called a "little finger break" to cut the cards easily at a particular spot (Step 5). The key to this trick is the smooth sequence of actions: after spreading the ten cards, square up the packet and cut them (at the break) so it appears you simply separated the two colors and then put the red ones underneath the black ones. Without pausing, turn the packet facedown and spread out the top five cards, (mis)calling them all red cards. This whole sequence takes only a few seconds.

STEP 4. Hold the packet of ten cards faceup in the dealing position. Allow the spectator to watch as you fan the top five red cards while counting to five. Continue fanning and counting the five black cards.

STEP 5. Hold the cards fanned between your hands as if you were playing a card game (a). You are now going to perform a special cut. As smoothly as you can, slip your little finger above the third card from the bottom while squaring up the cards (b). Hold this space as if it were the space between the red cards and the black ones.

Step 5a

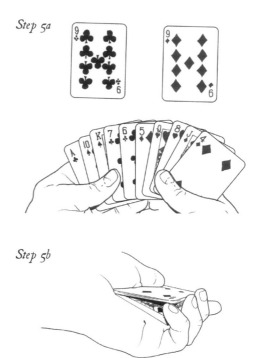

STEP 6. Cut the packet at the space and place the black cards on top of the red cards. Square up the packet. (At this point, there are three black cards, followed by five red cards, then two black cards, all faceup.)

Step 5b

STEP 7. Turn the packet facedown. Fan out the top five cards, calling them red cards. Place them facedown in a pile below the red leader card. You can actually flash or show the face card briefly to reinforce that these are indeed red cards. Do the same with the remaining cards, calling them black cards. Place them facedown below the black leader card.

STEP 8. Switch the leader cards so the red is now on the left and the black is on the right. Tell the spectator that the cards will want to associate with their correct leaders.

STEP 9. Turn over the top card of each pile, showing that the cards have indeed followed their leaders. Drop them faceup beneath each pile as you turn the cards over. Then turn over the next card of each pile, showing that they also have followed their leaders.

STEP 10. Now tell the spectator that, to make things more interesting, you will switch the two facedown piles and see if this continues to work. Turn over the remaining cards, one at a time. The spectator will see that they have also followed the leader cards.

THE ENVELOPE, PLEASE!

This card trick is easy to do—but it is truly awesome.
The only explanation is that you are clairvoyant!

EFFECT: The spectator shuffles the deck and places it on the table. You hand over a sealed envelope that contains a prediction. The spectator turns over the top card of the deck, and it matches the prediction.

NEEDED: A deck of cards, an envelope, a piece of paper, and a pen or pencil.

SECRET AND SETUP: You will hide a card (your prediction) behind the envelope; it will be added back to the top of the deck when you give the envelope to the spectator. Ahead of time, write on a piece of paper the name of the card you will hide. This will be your prediction. It can be any card—let's say it is the Six of Hearts. Fold this paper and put it in an envelope and seal it. Then remove from the deck the card that matches your prediction—in this case, the Six of Hearts. Put the card face out behind the envelope. You can keep the envelope and card in your pocket until you are ready to present this trick or you can have the envelope on the table (with the card hidden underneath).

STEP 1. Give the spectator the deck to shuffle. While he's doing this, take out the envelope with the card hidden behind it. Hold the envelope (along with the hidden card) in your right hand, with your hand by your side. Don't say anything about the envelope yet.

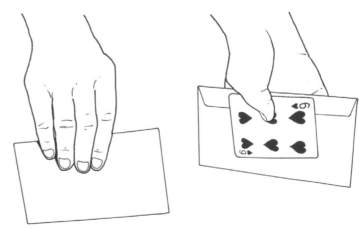

STEP 2. While the spectator is shuffling the deck, tell him that you had a feeling about a certain card. Further, tell him that you wrote the name of the card on a piece of paper, then sealed it in the envelope. Hold the envelope casually, keeping the Six of Hearts hidden.

STEP 3. When the shuffling is completed, have the spectator place the deck on the table. Now you simply place the envelope, along with the hidden card, on top of the deck. You are adding this card to the deck right in front of the spectator. He won't suspect that you've added the card. As you place the envelope (and card) down, say, "This is my prediction. It's still sealed. Pick it up and look it over."

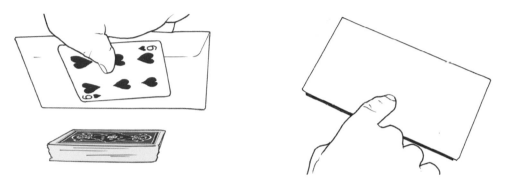

STEP 4. Ask the spectator to open the envelope and read the prediction inside.

STEP 5. The spectator opens the envelope and reads the prediction. If others are watching, ask him to read it out loud. The spectator will not know the significance of the prediction.

STEP 6. Say, "You don't know what I was predicting. I was predicting which card would be on top of the deck after you finished shuffling. Turn over the top card and take a look." Have the spectator turn over the top card.

 In a prediction trick like this, you would usually have the top card turned over first, then you would ask the spectator to open the envelope and read the prediction. Try the trick both ways and see which way you prefer to present it.

INSTANT SPELL

This is a quick trick—but still an awesome one.

EFFECT: The spectator "thinks" of any card, the deck is shuffled, she spells her card, and there it is!

NEEDED: A deck of cards.

SECRET AND SETUP: A six-card setup is required. This six-card setup, from the top down, is: Ten of Clubs, Six of Spades, Jack of Hearts, Eight of Spades, Nine of Diamonds, and Queen of Diamonds. Place nine cards on top of this six-card setup. Then place all fifteen cards on top of the deck. Thus, from the top of the deck down, there are nine indifferent cards followed by the six-card setup, beginning with the Ten of Clubs and ending with the Queen of Diamonds.

STEP 1. Shuffle, keeping the top stock of at least fifteen cards intact. Now all you have to do is force one of those six cards in the setup. This is all about timing. Practice, so you are comfortable completing the force with ease. Start dealing cards, singly and facedown, from your left to right hand, without reversing their order. That is, take the cards one under the other with your right hand. Take five or six cards this way, then say, "Oh, stop me whenever you like."

STEP 2. You've dealt another three or four cards as you say that sentence. Make the remark a little impatiently. Ninety-nine percent of the time, you'll be stopped at one of the vital cards (one of the six cards in the setup, beginning with the tenth card dealt). If not, don't panic. Let the spectator stop you anywhere, and do a different trick. For example, if the spectator stops you at a card that is not part of the setup group, just remove the next seven cards and present Lie Detector instead (page 14).

STEP 3. Show the spectator the stopped-at card (turn your head aside), and tell her to concentrate on it.

STEP 4. Put the right-hand cards back onto the deck so that all cards are as they were originally.

STEP 5. Do a shuffle, but retain the top stock. Hand the deck to the spectator and tell her to be sure to remember the card she pulled earlier. Remind her that the deck has been shuffled.

STEP 6. Have her name the card she chose earlier. Tell her to spell it from the top of the deck, one card at a time, including the word "of." Her card will fall on the final "s." After she finishes spelling, have her turn over the card.

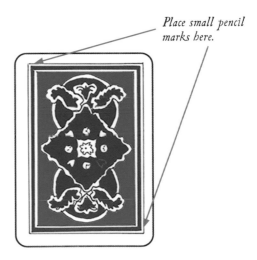

Place small pencil marks here.

You might try this tip: place small pencil marks on the back outer left and inner right corners of the Ten of Clubs, hidden so only you would notice (by marking both ends, you ensure that the mark is visible, no matter which direction the Ten of Clubs is in the deck).

Now you can simply glance at the mark to know the start of the six-card group of vital cards, and you will have more assurance that you will be among the six cards. As an alternative to dealing the cards hand to hand facedown, you can hold the deck up, with the faces toward your spectator. Your left thumb pushes off a group of cards until you see your mark; then, using your thumb and fingers underneath the spread, widely spread the next few cards and simply ask the spectator to remember a card. The spectator only really sees your setup cards. You must practice to get the timing down.

MIXED-UP ACES

Magically finding the four Aces in a shuffled deck is always an impressive feat; this trick is even more amazing because you are mixing cards faceup and facedown.

EFFECT: You cleanly divide the deck into two halves and turn one half faceup. You then shuffle the two halves together, so the deck is a mishmash of faceup and facedown cards. With a snap of the fingers, all the cards instantly correct themselves and are faceup, *except* for four cards: the four Aces!

NEEDED: A deck of cards.

SECRET: The four Aces are already reversed on the bottom of the deck. You also do a sneaky turnover just before shuffling. To prepare for the trick, place the four Aces reversed (faceup) on the bottom of the deck.

STEP 1. Bring out the deck of cards, but don't show the bottom of the deck with the reversed cards. Hold the deck in the left-hand dealing position.

STEP 2. Cut about half the deck of cards, lifting the top half by the ends with your right hand.

Step 2

STEP 3. Here's the sneaky move: you are going to turn over both halves at the same time. As your right hand is clearly rotating palm up, your left hand is *quickly and secretly* turning palm down.

Just place the left-hand packet on the table. Then place the right-hand packet on the table faceup, next to the first packet, in preparation for a riffle-shuffle. Say, "Once, when I was going to do a card trick for a guy, he asked to shuffle the deck first. Before I had a chance to stop him, he turned half the deck faceup and shuffled them into the facedown half, like this." (All attention should be directed to the right hand, which is turning faceup.)

STEP 4. The two halves are on the table. The left-hand packet looks like it is facedown, but it is actually faceup with the four facedown Aces on top. The right-hand packet is faceup. Now shuffle the two halves together, but you have to do this so that the spectator does not notice that the left-hand packet has faceup cards in it. Keep your hands close together during the shuffle and don't raise the corners too much. After the first shuffle, it doesn't matter.

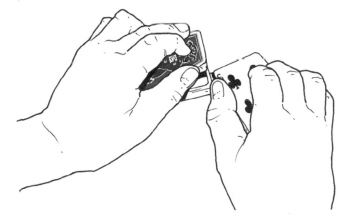

STEP 5. The spectator believes you are shuffling facedown cards into faceup cards. In fact, you are only mixing the facedown Aces into a faceup deck. Give the deck a cut, then perform some more shuffles and cuts. Ideally, during this process a facedown card will show; this impresses on the spectator the idea that the cards are really mixed faceup and facedown. You will want to shuffle multiple times at this point to ensure that the four Aces are distributed throughout the deck.

STEP 6. Say, "My challenger then put the deck in front of me with a malicious gleam in his eye and said, 'Now do a trick.'" The deck is now faceup on the table.

STEP 7. Tell the spectator, "I accepted the challenge." Pick up the deck and give it a little shake, and then ribbon spread it faceup on the table from left to right. Say, "So I corrected the deck so all the cards were the same way."

STEP 8. Wait for the spectator to notice that there are four facedown cards still in the spread. He will invariably question those. Say, "Oh . . . there's a reason for that." Push the four facedown cards forward, out of the spread, then turn each one over, revealing the four Aces.

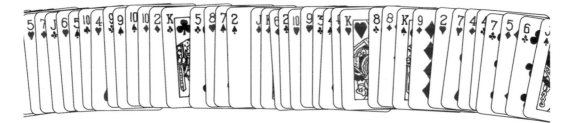

 The most influential close-up magician of the twentieth century was a gentleman named Dai Vernon. Known as "The Professor," Vernon came up with the plot used in this trick (faceup cards mixed with facedown cards that instantly correct themselves)—he called this plot "Triumph."

I WIN, YOU LOSE

You play a little head-to-head poker with the spectator, using just ten cards. You always win!

EFFECT: Ten cards are dealt from the deck into two five-card poker hands. Despite the fairness of the shuffling and dealing, you always have the better hand. For the finale, you allow the spectator to actually view the faces of the cards to decide on his hand. He will still lose.

NEEDED: A deck of cards. For the poker demonstration, you will use ten cards from the deck: three Aces, three Kings (or Queens), three Tens, and one Nine.

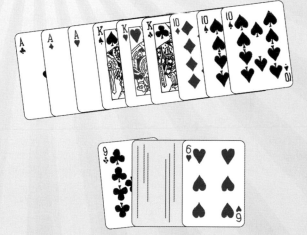

SECRET: When the cards are dealt, whoever has the Nine in his hand will lose. You make sure that the spectator ends up with the Nine each time.

STEP 1. Openly remove the three Aces, three Kings (or three Queens), and three Tens. Don't necessarily call attention to what the cards are, but it's okay if the spectator sees what you are doing. You don't sort these cards (the illustration is ordered so you can easily see which cards are being used). During the process of looking for these cards, secretly get a Nine to the top of the deck. Any Nine will do.

STEP 2. Say, "We are going to play a little head-to-head poker with these cards. I call this game 'I Win, You Lose' because I will always win." Hand the (nine) cards to the spectator to shuffle. Don't mention the number of cards, just let him assume that there are ten cards (not nine) that will be used for the poker hands.

STEP 3. After the spectator has mixed up the group of cards, take them back and place them on top of the deck. Then hand the deck to the spectator.

STEP 4. Say, "Please deal two five-card poker hands. It's just you and me." He should deal the first card to you, then deal alternately. The tenth card, which he deals to himself, will be the Nine. When he finishes dealing, you will announce: "Good! I win, you lose. Turn the cards over." Both of you will turn your hands over and, of course, you will win, since the spectator has the Nine.

STEP 5. Say, "Let's play again. I'll deal." Scoop up all the cards, making sure the odd card (the Nine) is on top this time. If you use the Nine to scoop up the others, it will get to the top naturally. You can also mix these cards up a little, but make sure the Nine stays or ends up on top. You deal the ten cards into two hands. Since the first card dealt to the spectator is the Nine, he will lose. After dealing, announce, "I win, you lose. Turn the cards over."

STEP 6. Scoop up the cards again, making sure the Nine is on top. Say, "This time we'll play draw poker." Spread the ten cards across the table facedown. "Who shall draw first?" It makes no difference who draws first. You keep an eye on the top card, which is the Nine. You each alternate taking cards. Since you would never pick the top card, the spectator most often ends up picking this from the group.

In the event you are left with the Nine, don't worry. Before the cards are turned over, simply add a new rule: "Let's gamble. You give me one of your cards, and I'll give you one of mine." You will, of course, give him your Nine. Or you could ask if the spectator would like to switch hands, or if he wants to trade several cards (all without looking at the faces).

STEP 7. As before, you announce, "I win, you lose." You both turn your hands up, and you win. Scoop up the cards and, as before, make sure the Nine is on top.

STEP 8. Say, "Let's play one more hand." Deal the first card to the spectator, then start to deal the second card to yourself, but stop just before placing it on the table. Turn to the spectator, show him the face of the card (don't look at it yourself), and say, "To be more fair, I'll let you decide: would you like this card or should I take it?" Keep doing this, showing the spectator the face of the card first (you don't look at the faces), then offering the spectator the choice of taking the card or not (until he has five cards). Remember, he didn't have the chance to pick his first card, which was the Nine.

STEP 9. Say, "I win, you lose." Turn over the two hands. Despite the spectator picking the cards he desired (usually he will end up with three of a kind), you win (typically with a full house).

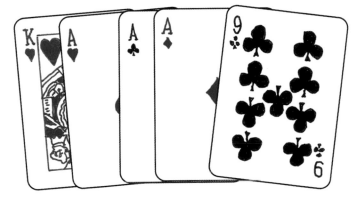

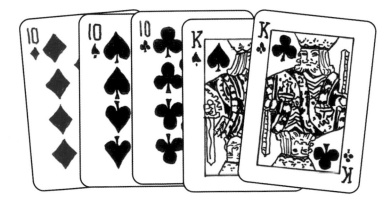

VALUE AND SUIT

Here's an awesome card trick where you never touch the cards.
It's simple but baffling.

EFFECT: A spectator shuffles a deck of cards and fans them toward you. You point to a card to have it removed and put aside facedown. The spectator then deals part of the deck into two piles. The top card of each pile is turned over, and the suit of one and the value of the other are combined and found to match the card previously set aside.

NEEDED: A deck of cards.

SECRET: You really don't know what the prediction card will be until the spectator fans the deck toward you. You first look at the top two cards of the deck—combined, they tell you which card you will tell the spectator to remove. These two cards will end up on top of the two piles that will be dealt.

STEP 1: Ask a spectator to shuffle the cards and then fan the deck so you can see the faces. Tell him that you will not touch the cards at all.

STEP 2: First look at the top two cards (on the left). Simply remember the value of the first card and the suit of the second. Don't clutter your mind with what the cards actually are, just remember the value of the first . . . then the suit of the second. This combination card will become your prediction, the card you will now have the spectator remove. In our example, the first card is the Six of Hearts and the second card is the King of Clubs. Your prediction card will be the Six of Clubs.

Sometimes the first two cards will not work. For example, if the first card is the Six of Hearts and the second card is another Heart suit, the prediction card would be the top card. But that card can't be removed, of course. If this happens, simply say to the spectator that you didn't see the card in your mind's eye, and have him cut the deck and start over.

STEP 3: Now, look back through the fanned deck for the prediction card, the Six of Clubs, in this example. When you see it, have the spectator remove it and put it facedown on the table.

Value   *Suit*

STEP 4: Ask the spectator to deal the cards into one pile on the table and to stop whenever he wishes. The original top two cards of the deck are now at the bottom of this pile. In order to get them to the top again, the cards must be dealt a second time.

STEP 5: After the spectator stops dealing, have him put the deck aside, and then have him pick up the pile of cards just dealt. Say, "Deal that packet into two piles, alternating left and right." Notice on which pile the final card was dealt. This will be the value card, the first one you will have turned over.

STEP 6: Say, "You shuffled and dealt the cards. Throughout this trick, I never touched the cards. You have ended up with two random piles of cards. Let's look at the top cards and see what they tell us." Point to the last card dealt and say, "We will use this card to indicate a value, or rank, of a card." Have the spectator turn it over (the Six of Hearts, in our example), and say, "Here's a Six." Ignore the suit; don't mention it. Point to the other pile and say, "This card will indicate a suit." Have the spectator turn that card over (the King of Clubs, in our example). Say, "Clubs . . . Six of Clubs!"

STEP 7: Say, "Remember that I had you remove a card at the very beginning. Turn it over."

PREMONITION

This trick works automatically, if you do it exactly as explained.

EFFECT: You state that you have a premonition, then you write it down and place it in the spectator's breast pocket. The spectator then chooses four random cards and you deal cards onto these, bringing each one "to ten." The spectator adds up the total of his four random cards, and the counted cards are replaced at the bottom of the deck. The spectator counts down to his number, and this card matches your written premonition.

NEEDED: A deck of cards, a pencil, and a scrap of paper.

SECRET: The predicted card is the card on the bottom of the deck. Math does the rest, but you need a full deck of fifty-two cards.

STEP 1. Glimpse the bottom card of the deck and remember it. Don't be obvious about this glimpse. You can give the deck a shuffle, keeping the known card in place.

STEP 2. Put the deck on the table. Then say that you have a premonition, a "feeling" about a certain card. On a small scrap of paper, write the name of the bottom card.

STEP 3. Take the two top cards from the deck, turn them face to face, and put the piece of paper between them. "This way I can't get near my written premonition again. We'll leave it here for safekeeping." Put the cards (and the sandwiched premonition) into your spectator's breast pocket—or have him sit on the sandwiched cards or put them under a book or some other object near the spectator.

STEP 4. Pick up the deck and give it a shuffle, keeping the bottom card on the bottom. Nonchalantly toss out five pairs of faceup cards. These are taken from the top and turned faceup as you toss them onto the table. You must place exactly ten cards on the table (but you don't want the counting to be obvious).

STEP 5. As you haphazardly toss the cards, say, "Please take any four of these cards."

STEP 6. After the spectator indicates four cards, pick up the remaining six cards and place them at the bottom of the deck. Spread the four cards in a horizontal row. Say, "You could have selected any cards, but these are the ones you wanted. I'll bring each card to ten."

STEP 7. Do exactly that, dealing and counting off the top of the deck. Let's assume the four cards are a Seven, a Three, a King, and an Ace. Point to the Seven. "That's a Seven—eight, nine, ten." Deal three cards, facedown, onto and overlapping the Seven as you count.

STEP 8. Point to the three-spot. Deal seven cards onto it, counting, "Four, five, six . . ." up to ten. Point to the King. "Pictures are already ten, so we'll leave it alone." Point to the Ace. "That's a one." Deal nine cards onto it, counting, "Two, three, four . . ." up to ten. The counting is done this way no matter what the cards are. On a nine-spot, you'd deal only one card. Any picture card is considered ten, and no cards are dealt onto it.

STEP 9. Say, "All right, would you add the four faceup cards for me?" Let the spectator total the four cards. "Twenty-one. Fine. Remember that number, please." Check his addition, of course.

STEP 10. Gather up *all* the tabled cards (turning them so they all face the same direction) and put them on the bottom of the deck. Then hand the deck to the spectator. "Please count down to the—what was the number again?—twenty-first card. Don't look at it; just place it aside, facedown."

STEP 11. Let the spectator do just that, dealing cards from the top, one by one, facedown, to the table. Have him place aside the last card—in this example, the twenty-first.

STEP 12. Say, "Now, I haven't come near you, or my written premonition, since we started with a shuffled deck, have I? Please remove my premonition, and read it out loud." He does.

STEP 13. Say, "Would you turn over that twenty-first card?" He does, proving that you can predict the future!

 Again, this trick works automatically. The important points: glimpse the bottom card without making it obvious. Place your written premonition between two cards (it won't work if you don't do this). You must place ten cards on the table, and all used cards must go to the bottom. The predicted card moves upward into position, mathematically and automatically. And always have the spectator read your premonition before he turns up the card.

ASHES ON THE ARM

What makes some card tricks truly awesome is the *revelation* of the selected card. This trick has one of the most amazing revelations of all. It's freaky!

EFFECT: A spectator selects a card and writes the name of the card on a scrap of paper while your back is turned. You turn around, light the paper on fire, and drop it in an ashtray. Then you take the cooled ashes and rub them on your forearm. *The name of the chosen card is revealed, written across your forearm.*

NEEDED: A deck of cards, a tube of lip balm (such as ChapStick), a pencil, a scrap of paper, an ashtray, and a lighter.

SECRET AND SETUP: The selected card is a forced card. This means that you control which card the spectator chooses. Before the presentation, unknown to others, you have written the card's initials on your forearm with the lip balm. To prepare the trick, select the card you want to use (the force card) and place it on the top of the deck. Let's say you decide on the Three of Diamonds. Prepare your arm by writing the abbreviated name of the card with the lip balm. In our example, you would write the number "3" and the outline of the diamond shape. The writing will be invisible, but the lip balm is slightly sticky. When you rub ashes on your forearm, they will adhere to this secret writing.

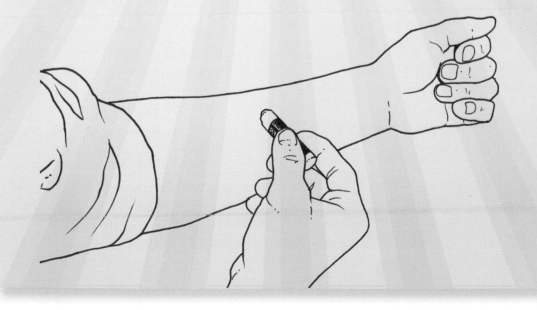

STEP 1. There are several ways to "force" a spectator to select a certain card. You are going to use a simple but clever one called the Crisscross Force. Remember that the card to be forced (the Three of Diamonds, in our example) is on the top of the deck. Place the deck on the table in front of the spectator. Ask him to cut the cards at any point. Point to a spot on the table (close to the deck), and he'll place his half in that position. By pointing in this way, you also make sure he does not complete the cut.

STEP 2. Pick up the original bottom half and place it on top of the spectator's half in a crisscross position, saying, "Let's mark the cut." Now you create a little "time misdirection," meaning you do something or talk for a moment or ask the spectator a question before continuing.

Step 2

STEP 3. After taking attention away from the deck for a moment, lift off the upper half (the crossed portion) of the deck with your right hand, and with your left hand point at the top card of the lower half. This is the original top card (the force card). Say, "Look at the card you cut to." Then have the spectator put the card back, and you replace your half on top.

STEP 4. Say to the spectator, "I want you to focus on that card. To reinforce the image of the card, I'd like you to write the name of it on this piece of paper." Hand the spectator a pencil and a slip of paper. Tell him, "I won't look," and turn your head or turn around. Then ask him to fold the paper so you can't see what he has written.

Place the deck aside, as it will not be needed.

STEP 5. Take the folded paper and light it at one end. Drop it into the ashtray and allow it to burn completely. Wait about thirty seconds or so until the ashes are cool. Please be careful here!

STEP 6. Roll up your shirtsleeve to expose the arm on which you previously wrote with lip balm.

STEP 7. Pick up the flakes of ash and drop them on your forearm. Rub the ashes gently across your arm, so the ashes stick to the lip balm. The name of the card will magically appear. Be prepared for gasps from your spectator when he sees the name of his card.

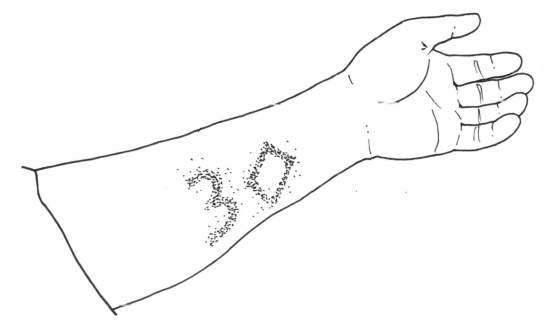

 # SLEIGHT OF FOOT

Magicians have different ways of presenting this classic trick—
but all involve the cunning use of a few grains of salt.

EFFECT: Without touching the cards, you find the spectator's selection with a simple tap of your foot while the deck of cards is on the floor.

NEEDED: A deck of cards and several grains of salt.

SECRET AND SETUP: Without your audience's knowledge, you will use a few grains of salt to locate a spectator's card. You will need to get a few grains of salt on your index fingertip. This is a perfect trick to do around the dinner table, as salt is generally available. You might place a few grains of salt nearby on the table (no one will notice this). When it's time to do this trick, press your fingertip firmly onto the salt so that grains adhere to your finger. You are going to secretly place some of these grains on top of the selection while pointing to it.

STEP 1. Hand the deck to a spectator to shuffle. Then divide the deck into three or four piles on the table.

STEP 2. Have the spectator remove a card from the center of one of the piles, look at it, and remember it. (You can turn your back while the spectator selects the card, if you prefer.) Have the spectator place his selection on top of any of the piles.

STEP 3. You are now going to instruct the spectator to replace the piles, one on top of another. But when you do so, you will add a few grains of salt to the top of the selection. Here's how: point to the pile with the selection and instruct the spectator to place any

Sprinkle salt on top of selected card.

of the piles on top of this. While pointing, tap the card slightly to indicate it as you tell him to place the piles on top of this card. When you tap the card, a few grains of salt will remain. You don't actually have to touch the cards, either. You can extend your fingertip over the pile with the selection; rub your thumb against your fingertip, dislodging some of the salt so that it falls directly onto the chosen card. You should practice this to determine just the right amount of salt needed (around half a dozen grains should be sufficient).

STEP 4. The spectator replaces the piles in any order, until the entire pack is assembled.

STEP 5. Ask the spectator to place the deck on the floor.

STEP 6. With the side of your shoe, strike the side of the deck with a firm blow. The cards will slide apart most dramatically at the point where the salt is. The grains of salt act like ball bearings. This will be your key. Remove the card just below this break. Ask for the name and reveal it.

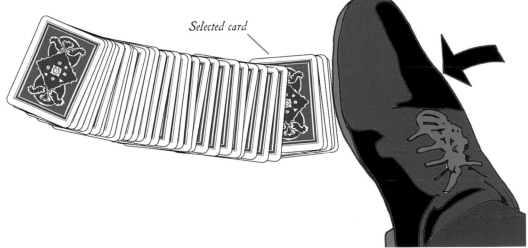

Selected card

 Practice this so you know how much salt to use and how hard to tap the deck with your shoe. Newer, slippery cards work best— and you only need to give the deck a little tap with your shoe. However, older cards require a stronger tap. If you tap too much, the cards might spray across the floor.

If you are not around a dinner table with readily available salt, you will need to prepare by placing a little salt in your pocket. You can reach into your pocket and get a few grains of salt onto your fingertip. You could also try using a few grains of sand instead of salt. One magician does this and uses a golf putter to tap the deck instead of his foot.

THOUGHT ECHO

Thought Echo is an awesome mental trick—two spectators pick cards in the fairest manner, and you find them immediately! This trick will fool even many magicians—it's truly diabolical in its method.

EFFECT: The deck is shuffled by two spectators (#1 and #2). They choose random cards while the pack is out of your hands. The deck is gathered, squared, and given back to you. Without hesitation, you immediately find both cards.

NEEDED: A deck of cards.

SECRET AND SETUP: A slight setup does the work. Arrange eleven indifferent cards on top of the deck, followed by the Ace through King of Clubs in numerical order, then the remainder of the deck.

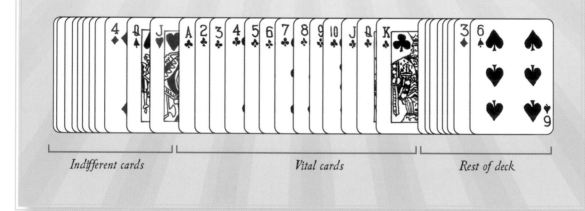

Indifferent cards   Vital cards   Rest of deck

STEP 1. Bring out the prepared deck. Place it facedown in front of Spectator #1. Tell him to cut about one-third of the deck off the top and place this packet to the right of the deck (Packet C).

STEP 2. Then have Spectator #2 cut about half the remainder and place this packet to the left (Packet A). The bottom of the deck is between the two packets (Packet B). The illustration shows the situation from your view.

A   B   C

STEP 3. Ask Spectator #1 to pick up Packet C, on the right (the original top third). Have him shuffle it thoroughly and replace it on the table. Then have him look at the top card of the packet and replace this card on top of the packet.

STEP 4. Turn to Spectator #2 and say, "Look at the top card of your packet, also." As you talk, gesture toward the packet on your left (Packet A) so that he knows to look at the top card of that packet.

STEP 5. Ask Spectator #1 to shuffle the middle packet (Packet B) and replace it on the table. As an apparent afterthought, turn to Spectator #2 and say, "You shuffle your packet, too."

STEP 6. Have the middle packet (Packet B) replaced on top of Packet C, on the right. When directing the spectator to do this, refer to the "shuffled" Packets B and C.

STEP 7. Have Spectator #2 replace his shuffled Packet A on top of all. Ask the spectator to square the deck.

STEP 8. The location of the two cards now seems impossible because all three packets have been fairly cut and shuffled. You have not handled the deck up to this point. Take the deck and fan the cards with the faces toward you. Look through the top third for the lowest-value Club. This will be

Top of deck

Spectator #2's card. In our example, this is a Nine of Clubs. You can remove this card and place it facedown on the table, or move it to the top of the deck in readiness for the revelation at the end (Step 11).

STEP 9. The *value* or number of this card clues you to the location of Spectator #1's card. You simply add ten to the value of Spectator #2's card to know the position of the other card. In this example, your sum would be nineteen.

STEP 10. Holding the deck facing you, count from the bottom (the first card facing you) the number of cards you determined in Step 9. In this example, you'd count nineteen cards in from the bottom. The nineteenth card is the one chosen by Spectator #1.

Count to 19th card

STEP 11. The easiest way to reveal the two chosen cards is to remove them and place them facedown on the table. Or, while you are looking through the deck for the cards, you could say to the spectators, "Please concentrate on your card." Present this as if you can read the spectators' thoughts. Reinforce that the two spectators cut and shuffled the cards and selected two cards. They replaced the cards. You did not handle the cards. Ask each spectator the name of his card and turn each card over.

THE CARD FROM THE BLACK HOLE

This is an awesome trick, in which a card vanishes from a sealed envelope!

EFFECT: Five cards are shown to the spectator, who writes down each card's name on a piece of paper. These cards are placed in an envelope. You then remove four of the cards while the spectator crosses off each name. The remaining card is sealed in the envelope, which acts like a black hole. The envelope is torn to pieces—the card has vanished. It reappears from your pocket or from another unlikely location.

NEEDED: Five cards total: the double-faced card (gimmicked card), the regular Nine of Spades, and three regular cards; also, an opaque envelope, a piece of paper, and a pen or pencil.

SECRET AND SETUP: A special card is utilized: the double-faced card (Queen of Hearts on one side and Nine of Spades on the other). Put the Nine of Spades facedown in your pocket and place the double-faced card in the deck, near the bottom, with the Queen showing.

STEP 1. Before you start the trick, the setup must be in place: the regular Nine of Spades should be in your pocket facedown (see the tip on page 63). Have the double-faced card near the bottom of the deck with the Queen showing (the regular Queen of Hearts should not be near the bottom of the deck; you don't want the spectator to notice two of them). You state that you will be using five cards, but you will only, in fact, remove four cards. The spectator should not suspect this, so remove them casually without arousing suspicion. Arrange the four cards in a packet so that they are faceup and you have the double-faced card on top with the Queen of Hearts side up.

STEP 2. Hold the packet of cards faceup in the dealing position. Tell the spectator to number the piece of paper from one to five.

STEP 3. Take the Queen with your fingers on the top and your thumb below, as shown. Pivot the card toward the spectator so he sees the Queen (a). As you do so, ask him to write down the name of this first card next to the number one. Place the card at the bottom of the packet, turning it over so that the side with the Nine of Spades faces up (b and c). When you do this, make sure that the spectator does not see the Nine of Spades.

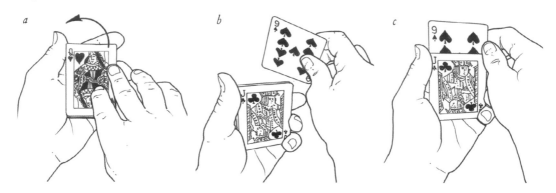

STEP 4. Call out the name of the next card, as you use the same move to show the card and then place it on the bottom of the packet. Have the spectator write its name beside the next number.

STEP 5. Repeat this procedure until you get to the last card—the double-faced card with the Nine of Spades showing. Show this card and ask the spectator to write "Nine of Spades" next to the number five on the list. Leave this card faceup on top of the packet of cards in your hand.

STEP 6. The spectator will have the names of five cards written down, although you actually have only four cards in your hand. Place the cards in the envelope with the Nine of Spades facing you. Hold the envelope so that the spectator cannot see into it. Say to the spectator, "This envelope is the link to a black hole."

STEP 7. Withdraw the cards, one by one, showing the faces to the spectator. Begin with one of the regular cards. Place it faceup on the table while asking the spectator to cross off its name from the list.

STEP 8. Next, remove the double-faced card with the Queen of Hearts side faceup and place it on the table. Ask the spectator to cross its name from the list.

STEP 9. Continue with the two remaining cards. As each card is brought out, have its name crossed off the list. The spectator will think you have one card left in the envelope—the Nine of Spades, which has not been crossed off the list. The envelope will, in fact, be empty.

STEP 10. Seal the envelope, apparently trapping the Nine of Spades inside. Emphasize that the Nine of Spades is still in the sealed envelope. Tell the spectator that you will cause it to transport to another location. Tear the envelope into pieces and throw the pieces into the trash.

STEP 11. Announce that you will retrieve the card from the other side of the black hole. With a magical flourish, remove the (regular) Nine of Spades from your pocket and show it to the spectator.

 When the trick is over, be sure to scoop up the cards so no one will learn the secret of the double-faced card.

Instead of keeping the regular Nine of Spades in your pocket, you might try placing it somewhere else nearby, such as under a book on the table, inside a wallet or purse, or under the cushion of the seat where the spectator is sitting. This trick is known as a "transposition"—a card disappears from one location, only to be found elsewhere. The magical effect is enhanced when the card is found someplace away from the magician.

BLIND LOCATION

Here's a trick where the spectator finds her own
card while holding the deck behind her back.

EFFECT: The spectator chooses a card. Then, while the deck is behind her back, she reverses a card and inserts it anywhere in the deck. Amazingly, the card she reversed is found right next to her chosen card: the spectator has located her card herself!

NEEDED: A deck of cards and the double-backed card.

SECRET AND SETUP: You use a special (gimmicked) card: a double-backed card. This card has a back on both sides that matches the deck. You hide this double-backed card under your belt at your back (or slip it inside the top of your pants) before starting the trick.

STEP 1. Ask a spectator to shuffle the cards and let her cut the pack into two even packets, handing you one and keeping the other herself.

STEP 2. Say, "I want you to place your packet behind your back." To show what you want her to do, place your packet behind your back.

STEP 3. While your packet is behind your back, add the double-backed card from under your belt (or wherever you have it) to the top of your packet. Say, "I want you to choose any card from the packet behind your back and look at it and remember it. Then replace it on top of your packet." Again, illustrating what you want the spectator to do, bring forward the bottom card, look at it (you don't have to remember it, though), and replace it behind your back. Say, "When you return it, add it to the top of your packet." However, when you return your card to your packet, you do not add it to the top of your packet. Instead, put it reversed on the bottom of your packet.

STEP 4. You now bring forward your packet and ask the spectator to do the same. Put your packet on top of the spectator's. This brings the card you reversed immediately above the spectator's card.

STEP 5. Say, "Now your card is buried in the middle. Place the deck behind your back."

STEP 6. While the deck is behind the spectator's back, continue: "Take off the top card, turn it faceup, and push it into the pack." (Here is what is happening: the spectator is actually taking the double-backed card and reversing it before pushing it into the deck.)

STEP 7. After the spectator does this, have her bring the deck forward and place it facedown on the table.

STEP 8. Remind the spectator that her selection was buried in the middle of the deck somewhere, and while it was behind her back, she reversed a card and shoved it into the deck at a random location. Spread the cards facedown. Point to the faceup card. This is supposedly the one that the spectator reversed.

STEP 9. Remove the card adjacent (just below) the reversed card. Ask for the name of the selected card; turn it over to show that the spectator actually located her own card.

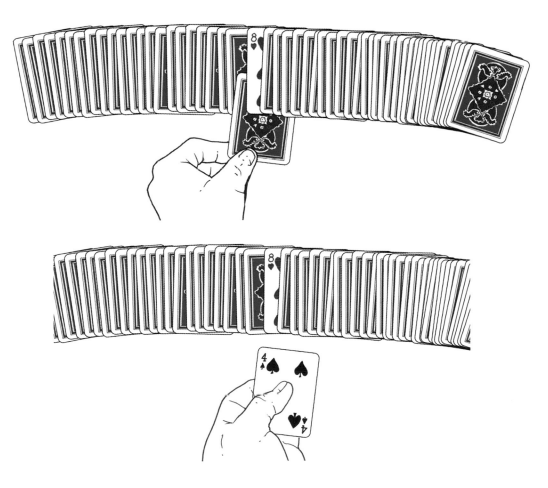

STRETCHING THE QUEEN

This is a quick effect using only three cards.

EFFECT: The Queen of Hearts is placed faceup between two facedown cards. You talk about the Queen's courtly elasticity. Grasping the Queen from both ends, you stretch the card to almost twice her length. You then compress her back to her original size.

NEEDED: Three cards: the double-faced card (gimmicked card), a regular Queen of Hearts, and a regular Nine of Clubs.

SECRET AND SETUP: A special card is utilized: the double-faced card (Queen of Hearts on one side and Nine of Spades on the other). To set up the trick, place the double-faced card, Nine of Spades showing, near the bottom of the deck. Also make sure that the Queen of Hearts and the Nine of Clubs are positioned toward the bottom of the deck.

STEP 1. You will begin the trick by removing the three cards from the deck: the special double-faced card (with the Nine of Spades showing), the regular Queen of Hearts, and the Nine of Clubs. These should be near the bottom of the deck, not necessarily together. (Either remove the regular Nine of Spades from the deck, or have it near the top. You do not want the spectator to notice that there is another Nine of Spades in the deck.)

STEP 2. Tell the spectator that you want to use three cards: a Queen and two spot-cards. Spread the deck faceup in your hands to remove the three cards. Act as if it really doesn't matter which cards you choose. You simply happen to be removing the two black Nines and the Queen of Hearts. The spectator will not suspect that the Nine of Spades you are removing is a special card. Put the deck aside.

STEP 3. Arrange the cards faceup in your left hand with the Nine of Clubs on the bottom near your palm, the Nine of Spades (the double-faced card) in the middle, and the Queen of Hearts showing on top. Then square up the cards and hold them in your left hand.

STEP 4. Hold the cards level to the ground. With your left thumb, deal the Queen of Hearts into your right hand. Turn both hands palm down, showing the backs in both hands while hiding the other side of the special double-faced card. Turn your hands palm up, returning to the original position. With your left hand, spread the Nine of Spades over to the right about one inch.

STEP 5. With your right hand, turn the Queen facedown and insert it between the two faceup Nines. Square up the packet and turn it over in your left hand so the Nines are facedown.

STEP 6. Tell the spectator: "The Queen of Hearts has a special quality. It's called 'courtly elasticity,' and it means she can stretch." Keep the cards level to the ground and hold them on the sides with your fingertips as shown (a). With your right thumb on top and fingers below, slide the bottom card (the double-faced card with the Queen showing) upward about half an inch (b). Then, from the other end of the packet, pull the next card—the regular Queen—downward about half an inch (c). Continue pulling the double-faced card and the regular Queen of Hearts until the Queen looks like she is stretched to almost twice her length.

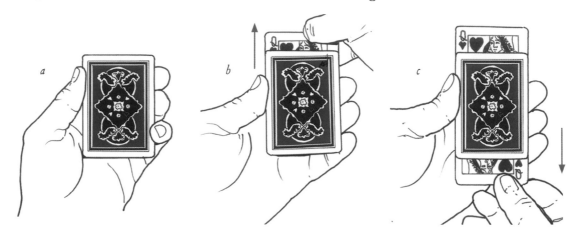

STEP 7. Once the effect is appreciated (a few seconds), with your right hand, push both ends of the stretched Queen together, collapsing the card into a squared-up, facedown packet.

STEP 8. To prove to the spectator that all is fair, turn the packet over in your left hand and spread it to show the two Nines and a facedown card. Pull the facedown card out, show that it is the Queen, and drop it on the table. Square the two cards in your left hand and turn your left-hand palm down, showing the back of the Nine of Clubs. Then turn your left-hand palm up

again and drop the Nine of Spades (the double-faced card) onto the table with the Nine of Spades showing, then again show the back of the Nine of Clubs with your left hand. Finally, scoop up all the cards with the Nine of Clubs, and put them back with the deck. (Of course, you must not let the spectator examine the cards.)

COLOR SEPARATION

This astounding miracle with cards will
amaze even the magicians who see it!

EFFECT: The deck is riffle-shuffled and shown completely mixed. You then deal the cards into two equal piles. The spectator takes one half, you take the other. The spectator deals her cards faceup, with the red cards in a pile on the table and the black cards in a pile next to the red cards. You deal your cards facedown but diagonally opposite to those the spectator is dealing. At the end, you reveal that all the colors have separated.

NEEDED: A deck of cards.

SECRET AND SETUP: This trick is based on a fascinating mathematical principle: the Gilbreath Principle, named after Norman Gilbreath. Given the setup, even after the cards are riffle-shuffled, certain properties of the outcome are mathematically guaranteed. In this trick, you begin with a deck that has alternating red and black cards. Prepare the deck by separating the red-suited cards from the black-suited cards. Set them up in an alternating arrangement (red, black, red, black, etc.). Put the deck back in its case, and you are ready to begin.

STEP 1. Remove the case from your pocket. Take the cards out and place them facedown on the table. Say, "You are about to see something quite remarkable." As you talk, cut the deck a few times, replacing the cut each time (this does not disturb the red-black arrangement).

STEP 2. Hand the deck to someone who knows how to riffle-shuffle. If you're not sure the person can shuffle this way, do it yourself. Give the deck a good riffle-shuffle. Turn the deck faceup on the table and ribbon spread the cards for a moment. Say, "The deck is completely mixed." (Amazingly, after the riffle-shuffle, the deck will still be organized so that, if cards are grouped into consecutive pairs, each pair will have one black card and one red card. In the presentation that follows, you will separate these pairs so that the black cards end up together and the red cards end up together.)

STEP 3. Look at the faceup spread of cards and find any two red or two black cards that have come together. There will usually be five or six pairs like this—look at the illustration and notice, for example, that the Jack of Hearts and Ace of Hearts make such a pair. In picking up the spread, separate the pair and cut the deck at this location. You can do this by picking up the bottom section first and then the remaining cards, placing them faceup on top of the first portion. Now turn the deck facedown.

STEP 4. Say, "We will need two groups of cards." Deal the deck facedown into two piles, one card to your left and the next to the right, alternating until the cards have been dealt. There will be twenty-six cards in each pile when you finish.

STEP 5. Ask the spectator: "Will you please pick up either of these piles and hold it in your hand, ready to deal?" Pick up the other pile and say, "I'm going to ask you to deal your cards faceup, one at a time, separating the red cards from the black ones. If the card is black, place it to your left. If it is red, place it to your right. As you deal each card, I will deal one facedown, but diagonally, opposite to your pile."

Step 6

X  Y

A  B

STEP 6. The spectator begins to deal her cards, placing the red-suited cards to her right (**X**) and the black-suited ones to her left (**Y**). For every black card she deals to her left (**Y**), you deal a facedown card diagonally opposite to your left (**A**). If she deals a red card to her right (**X**), you deal a facedown card to your right (**B**). Say, "I shall attempt to match you card for card by color."

STEP 7. Both of you now deal as described. At the completion of the deal, you each have two piles in front of you. Say, "Something unbelievable has happened." Turn each of her faceup piles over and place them on top of the facedown piles directly below them. Pile **X** will go on top of pile A; pile Y on top of pile B.

STEP 8. Turn each pile faceup and spread the cards. The red cards are in one pile, the black cards in the other.

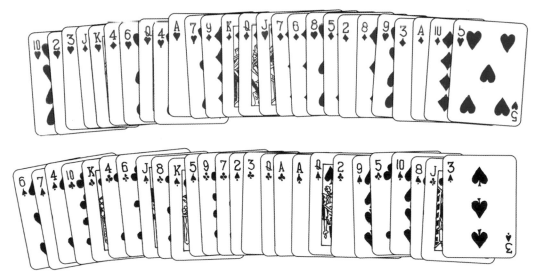

DOUBLE CARD PREDICTION

In this trick, you predict two cards that the spectator will find!

EFFECT: You write the names of two cards on a piece of paper, fold it, and give it to the spectator to keep. The spectator then shoves a facedown card anywhere into a faceup deck. The deck is turned over and spread. The spectator sees her reversed card and removes the cards on each side of the reversed card, turning them over. She then unfolds the piece of paper to read that you predicted exactly those cards.

NEEDED: A deck of cards, a double-backed (gimmicked) card, a piece of paper, and a pen or pencil.

SECRET AND SETUP: The double-backed card is the secret to this trick, along with a three-card setup. For the setup, take any two cards (these will be your prediction cards) and put a card faceup (reversed) between them. Put these three cards on top of the deck, with the prediction cards facedown. Then put the double-backed card on top of this. Thus, from the top down, you have the double-backed card, followed by one prediction card, then a card that is faceup, then the other prediction card. Write the names of the two cards on a piece of paper and fold it. If you will be able to remember the names of these two prediction cards later, you can wait to write them until the beginning of the trick; at that time, write the names on a piece of paper in front of the spectator, but do not show her the names.

STEP 1. Begin the trick by handing the spectator the folded piece of paper with the names of the prediction cards for safekeeping. You could also seal the piece of paper in an envelope and give the spectator the envelope.

STEP 2. Put the deck with the setup facedown on the table. Riffle-shuffle the cards, keeping the four top cards in position and covering up the pack well enough with your hands so the faceup card near the top won't be noticed. You can also simply turn the cards faceup and casually spread them, showing that the cards are well mixed. Remember not to spread the cards near the top, which would expose your setup.

STEP 3. With the deck facedown in your left hand, take off the top card (the double-backed card) with your right hand. Then flip the deck faceup. If you can't flip over the deck with one hand, just put the double-backed card on the table first.

STEP 4. Hand the double-backed card that you just removed to the spectator and invite her to thrust it anywhere in the faceup pack. Push the pack forward and have her do this quickly, so she will have no chance of turning the card over.

STEP 5. Give the spectator the deck and have her cut the pack, then turn it facedown and spread it on the table. One reversed card is visible and is naturally believed to be the card just inserted by the spectator.

STEP 6. Point to the reversed card and say, "You shoved this card in some random spot in the deck. Please remove the card above it and also the card below it. Let's see which two cards you found." The spectator removes the cards adjacent to the reversed card and turns them faceup.

STEP 7. Ask the spectator to now remove the piece of paper (or envelope) that you gave her at the beginning of the trick. She opens it to read that you predicted both cards!

FURTHER THAN THAT

This is one of my favorite card tricks. It is very entertaining, and it requires no sleight of hand. The title of the trick plays an important part in the presentation, since you will be repeating it throughout.

EFFECT: The spectator selects a card (the Ten of Spades). You will reveal the identity of the card after "listening" to the deck when you riffle a corner. But the trick goes *further than that*. You then find the selection. Still, the trick goes *further than that*. You also find the other Tens and a set of Spades. And, the trick goes *further than that*. You end up showing a royal flush!

NEEDED: A deck of cards.

SECRET AND SETUP: The secret is in the setup, and you will use a special mathematical technique to force the selection of a particular card. You will be forcing the spectator to select the Ten of Spades.

You are going to arrange a setup of fourteen cards and place it on top of the deck. Begin by removing eleven of the Spades (every one except the Two and Three of Spades) and all the Tens from the deck. Now arrange these as follows (from the top of the deck down): six Spade cards (the Four through Nine) in mixed order, then a red Ten, Ten of Clubs, the other red Ten, followed by the Ten of Spades, Ace of Spades, King of Spades, Queen of Spades, Jack of Spades. Place the prearranged deck back in the card case, so you are ready to perform.

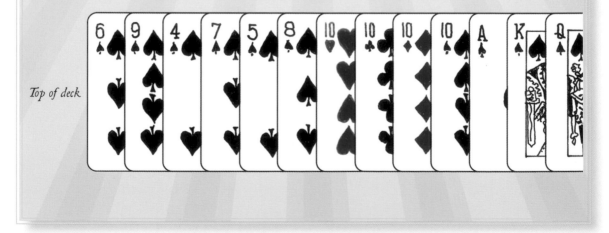

Top of deck

STEP 1. To present the effect, remove the deck from its case and shuffle the deck casually without disturbing the stack on the top. Tell the spectator, "This card trick has a name—it's called *Further Than That*."

STEP 2. Spread the cards facedown and say, "Most magicians will have you pick a card from the deck, like this." Close up the spread and turn the deck faceup. Spread them again (without revealing the prearranged setup at the top), and say, "Or like this." (Briefly spreading the deck faceup reinforces—without saying so—that the deck is mixed and there's no setup.)

STEP 3. Close up the deck, turn it facedown again, hold it in the left-hand dealing position, and say, "But this trick goes *further than that*. I am going to have you select a card by picking a position in the deck. Pick a number, say, between ten and twenty." (This is the start of the mathematical 10–20 Force.) Let's assume that the spectator chooses fifteen (as an example). You count aloud while dealing openly and distinctly fifteen cards into a facedown pile on the table. Place the balance of the deck down.

STEP 4. Point to the top card of the pile (the last card dealt) and say, "Most magicians would have you look at this card." Then say, "But this trick goes *further than that*. The number fifteen has two digits, a 'one' and a 'five.' If we add them together, we get six." Pick up the pile on the table and count off six cards into a new facedown stack on the table. Have the spectator look at the top card of this stack and replace it (it will be the Ten of Spades because of the mathematical force). Counting twice, as instructed, will always end with the tenth card from the top of the deck, which is the Ten of Spades. Place the balance of the first pile that you have in your hand on top of the replaced selection, then take the entire group of fifteen cards and drop them on top of the rest of the deck.

STEP 5. Pick up the pack, spread the cards, and say, "Most magicians would spread the cards and try to find your card. But this trick goes *further than that*." Square the deck, hold it in your left hand, bring it up to your ear, and riffle the corner of the deck with your thumb (listening to the sound). Say, "I can tell by the sound that you chose a black card." The spectator should acknowledge that it is a black card. Again, listen to the cards and say that the suit is Spades. Continue, gradually revealing the identity of the chosen card: you say it is a spot card, and then finally that it is the Ten of Spades.

STEP 6. The spectator thinks the trick is over (and that it is a pretty weak effect, too). However, you say, "Most tricks would end right here. But this trick goes *further than that*." Hold the deck in dealing position in your left hand. "Since your card was the Ten of Spades, I can find it by spelling. I'll spell 'T-E-N' here." Deal a card for each letter into an overlapping row on the left. "And I'll spell 'S-P-A-D-E-S' over here." As you talk, deal a card for each letter in a separate overlapping row on the right. Pause, point to the top card of the deck, and say, "And the next card is the Ten of Spades." Turn over the top card to reveal it. Pause. Drop the card faceup onto the table next to the other two rows of cards. The spectator will think the trick is over.

STEP 7. Say, "Most tricks would end right here. But this trick goes *further than that*." Point to the group of three cards on the left and say, "Over here I spelled 'TEN.'" Turn the three cards faceup to show that they are indeed all Tens.

STEP 8. Point to the other group of six cards on the table and say, "And here I spelled 'SPADES.'" Turn these cards over to reveal that they are all Spades.

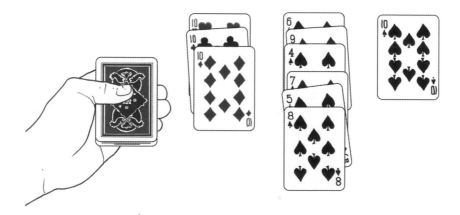

STEP 9. Again, pause and act like the trick is over. Your audience will be quite impressed with the trick at this point, but you say, "Most tricks would end right here." Pause. "But this trick goes *further than that*." Point to the Ten of Spades and say, "In a game of poker, you would have five cards in your hand." Deal four cards from the deck facedown on top of the Ten of Spades.

Then put the rest of the deck aside and (finally) say, "Most tricks would end right here, and so does this one . . ." (now turn over the group of four cards that you just dealt onto the Ten of Spades and spread them) "because you can't beat a royal flush in Spades."

 This trick utilizes the 10–20 Force, which forces the tenth card from the top of the deck to be selected (the Ten of Spades). The chosen number must be *between* ten and twenty. This mathematical force first saw print in 1935, but is believed to be much older. Its use here fits with the presentation since the trick goes "further than that," providing the justification for taking the two digits of the chosen number and adding them together. This final trick is indeed a reputation maker!

TRICK SOURCES AND INSPIRATION

Most of the tricks in *25 Awesome Card Tricks* have been developed over the years by me or by other members of the magical fraternity. These individuals are highly esteemed and should be credited. Origins of some principles are, for the most part, unknown.

Kings and Aces (p. 12)—this is an old trick. Richard Kaufman suggested the addition of the four indifferent cards at the beginning.

Lie Detector (p. 14)— this is based on Jim Steinmeyer's Nine Card Problem; David Solomon adapted it to a lie detector plot and streamlined it by using only seven cards.

Count Down Five (p. 17)—my mentor, Paul Swinford, taught this trick to me; I'm passing it along here.

Influential Cards (p. 20)—another legendary card man, Frank Garcia, often performed this trick.

Turn About (p. 22)—the trick comes from Francis Carlyle, one of the legendary card men of the twentieth century.

Awesome Prediction (p. 24)—this is a basic mathematical method of ending up at a certain card.

Spectator Cuts the Aces (p. 27)—this is a variation of a trick called Weigle Aces, first written up by Oscar Weigle in 1939.

Wanna Bet? (p. 30)—this is a classic trick used to win friendly bar bets.

Cheating at Cards (p. 32)—there are countless card tricks where you deal winning poker hands. Joshua Jay suggested this one, which features a plot showing how a card cheat can deal from the bottom of the deck.

Follow the Leader (p. 35)—this is a simplified version of a trick by Dai Vernon, published in 1938 in the "Card Stars" section of John Northern Hilliard's *Greater Magic*. The book is one of the classics of magic.

The Envelope, Please! (p. 38)—this is a blatant and straightforward approach in which a prediction card is added to the top of the deck. I learned it years ago.

Instant Spell (p. 40)—one of the many ways to reveal a card is through spelling. Harry Lorayne suggested this presentation.

Mixed-Up Aces (p. 42)—Dai Vernon, undoubtedly the most influential close-up magician of the twentieth century, developed the plot of this trick, which he called "Triumph."

I Win, You Lose (p. 45)—this is just one presentation of the magic principle called the Ten-Card Poker Problem.

Value and Suit (p. 48)—I first learned this trick from John Scarne, who wrote about it in the 1950s.

Premonition (p. 50)—another presentation by Harry Lorayne, this trick utilizes the mathematical principle of bringing cards "to ten."

Ashes on the Arm (p. 53)—this is a classic trick. Before there was lip balm, magicians wrote on their arm with a damp bar of soap, transferring the soap film to the arm.

Sleight of Foot (p. 56)—this trick was invented by Herbert Milton in the 1920s. He sold the secret for $25 (over $300 today).

Thought Echo (p. 58)—this remarkable trick comes from the genius of Sam Schwartz in the 1970s.

The Card from the Black Hole (p. 61)—I have to give credit to my old friend David Solomon for helping to develop this trick.

Blind Location (p. 64)—use of double-backed cards extends back to the 1860s, when Johann Hofzinser, called the Father of Card Magic, was using them to amaze audiences in Vienna.

Stretching the Queen (p. 66)—this is a good example of a "packet trick" that only uses a few cards along with a secret gimmicked card.

Color Separation (p. 69)—this is a presentation utilizing the Gilbreath principle. This underlying mathematical principle is one of the most intriguing discoveries in card magic.

Double Card Prediction (p. 72)—this use of the double-backed card was suggested by Jean Hugard in the 1950s.

Further Than That (p. 74)—several legends in magic have had a hand in this trick: Stewart James adapted the method; J. W. Sarles contributed; and Paul Swinford made further improvements.

ABOUT THE AUTHOR

John Railing is a Renaissance man with many interests and a varied business background. Widely considered one of the country's top close-up magicians, John performs regularly for an impressive roster of celebrities, entertainers, and leading corporate executives, and has performed for US presidents, foreign dignitaries, and heads of state from around the world. He currently performs tableside magic for diners at one of Chicago's premier restaurants, Swift & Sons.

With a specialty in sleight-of-hand magic, John combines engaging banter with an amazing repertoire of fascinating effects using cards, coins, and balls, in addition to an array of baffling illusions and mental tricks.

John cowrote and produced a series of top-selling magic sets called The Ultimate Magic Club, each with its own DVD, for Scholastic Books. Over the past fifteen years, he has consulted on film and stage productions, created illusions for trade fairs and corporate shows, and produced myriad products for the magic and toy industries. His work has included assisting David Copperfield with retail and magic for his new restaurant and entertainment complex; several licensed toys; magic-related candy packaging; magic books; and various other commercial projects involving 3-D printing, optical illusions, and puzzles.

He is actively involved with the Gathering 4 Gardner Foundation, which celebrates the work of the legendary recreational math author, the late Martin Gardner, with a playful and fun approach to mathematics, science, art, magic, games, and puzzles.

John lives in the Chicago area with his wife, Sheila, and their three children, Maxwell, Mia, and Macey.

ACKNOWLEDGMENTS

This book is a collaboration. I thank Tony Dunn for his wonderful illustrations. Special thanks to Nancy Hall and her team of editors and designers, especially Susan Lauzau and Tim Palin.